Publisher

Williams Commerce, LLC

Visit Our Website Williamscommerce1.com

ISBN: xxx-x-xxx-xxxxx-x

Table of Contents

Chapter 1: The Awkward Black Kid

Reflecting on one's childhood from the point of view of manhood can be an emotional and cruel thing to do. Still, I assume some therapy comes from turning back the pages. When I first think of growing up in the eighties in a small southern town, as the middle child in an African American family of five, nothing therapeutic comes to mind. I was an awkward kid to say the least. I was shy, but somehow not timid. I had a lot to say, just not a platform to say it. I was either interrupting "grown folks talking" which got me sent away, or my voice was merely drowned out in the crowd. As early as eight years of age, I wanted to be something different, someone different, and somewhere different.

I remember going to grade school daydreaming about having spiky blond hair and blue eyes like Kenny Sutherland. That way, I wouldn't be so shy. People would listen to me as they listened to him. They would love me, just as much as they loved Kenny. Yes, if only I were a White boy. That thought would bounce around my head like a pinball inside a pinball machine, my mind buzzing and lighting up as if I hit TILT when I thought of the attention I would receive from Kim Vann. She reminded me of the girls I would see on Nickelodeon. She was smart, funny, cute, and White.

This "whitewash" going on in my mind was the newest coat of paint from a vast history of white paint being splotched then worked into the grooves of my African heritage. The term "African American" had not been introduced yet, but a more accurate term to describe myself and my Black counterparts would be "American African." Heavy on the American, not so much of the African. So much in fact, that here I was, at the tender age of eight, secretly wanting to be White. I was halfway there, according to my peers.

"Why do you talk like that?" they would ask. "Like what?" I would say with a puzzled face. "Like that. Like a White person." This question, although it puzzled me, gave me some relief, some accolade from its suggestiveness. Could it be that I was gaining on Kenny Sutherland's heels? If only my nose were pointier and lips were thinner, I would think while looking in the mirror. If only my skin was lighter than the reddish pecan brown skin, I was born with. This "whiteness" I wanted was reinforced not only by the "whitewash" of American culture, but the negative reinforcement of my environment.

Ironically, the neighborhood I grew up in was predominantly Black. A middle-class suburb consisting of an older generation that worked hard and was rewarded handsomely for all their years of hard work. My parents did well for themselves and my siblings and I by moving us there in 1986. Although this neighborhood could easily be considered an ideal location to raise a family, an open wound of decay, the "ghetto," lay at the edges of this utopia. I was safe within the parameters of my neighborhood, my parents must have thought, having been surrounded by a host of aunts and uncles, first cousins and second cousins, faithful church devotees, hardworking homeowners, and the lot.

The day we moved into the neighborhood, I was introduced to the other neighborhood kids. I did not fit in as quickly as I wanted; you almost don't count when you're the new kid on the block. My older cousin Evon rescued me that day by initiating an impromptu game of superhero. The neighborhood boys, a little older than me, sprang into action, not letting the chance pass them by to cop a feel from my voluptuous kin, who seduced them as Wonder Woman. I remember her laughing as they groped her, tossing her to the ground. As if rehearsed, she lifted her bra up over her breast, displaying them to us. The image of her chest burned a permanent spot in my memory. It triggered a different feeling in my adolescent mind and body. The older boys made a huge fuss over her, pawing and clawing at her chest like a rabid hyena over a wounded gazelle. They seemed to know exactly what to do, and she seemed to enjoy it. I, however, was dumbfounded by what I was seeing. Not sure if it was right or wrong. I made my way back to my home while my young mind tried to make sense of all that had just happened.

Both sides of my family were large. We interacted with both sets quite often. All my older female cousins were gorgeous teenage girls who were the same age as my elder brother Vick. They all were in high school, and they all were the coolest to my cousins of the same age and me. My male cousins became my first friends. A set of cousins struck this balance: Stacy and Kaiden, siblings from my mother's sister Aunt Marcie. Aunt Marcie was a single mother, doing the best she could, raising kids in the projects by either working two jobs or getting welfare from the government. I had no idea what all this meant at the time. All I knew was I enjoyed visiting them in the projects. It was the opposite of my neighborhood and my home.

Stacy would put her brother and me on the spot whenever her friends or other family members were around. "Do the

Billie Jean!" she would say with a gleam in her eye and pride in her voice. Kaiden and I would rise to the occasion. Simulating all of Michael Jackson's dance routines, our audience would laugh and cheer at us. I wanted to die from all the attention. Even within our family, the difference in my reality and other Black kids' reality was shockingly different. "You guys are like the Cosbys." Stacy would say jokingly, but obviously seeing the difference in her home and ours.

My father could be funny at times, but he was no Heathcliff Huxtable. A high school dropout, somehow, he was able to land a good job and start his own business. He was a devoted father, husband, and a Christian, having a history of being this street hustler and basketball street legend that was unbeknownst to me at the time. My mother, who resembled Claire Huxtable, was hardworking and stern. She had a huge heart that had been hurt one time too many; it made her bitter and paranoid. The life she and my father made together was her happiness, her joy, her accomplishment. My siblings and I were jewels in her crown. My father was cool, calm, and collected. My mother was, for lack of a better word, overprotective.

One day, there was a huge birthday party for one of the neighbor's grandson. I was tentatively invited, yet I couldn't attend. My mother insisted on me staying in our backyard playing with my little sister Vivian. Being that I didn't quite fit in with the neighborhood guys, I was quite relieved by her demand. That is until the backlash happened while I was playing with my kid sister on our swing set in the backyard. The party was in full swing next door. The smell of a summertime cookout filled the air along with music and chatter of kids having fun during a water gunfight. I got an eyeful of the birthday party from a distance, then insults and derogatory gestures were shot in my direction. "Look at the faggot play with his sister!" one of the kids yelled. "Hey you, kiss my ass!" another taunted as he pulled down his pants and underwear and mooned me. They all laughed and continued to harass me. I was doubly beside myself. On one hand, I was repulsed by how they were acting, what they were saying, and the fact that I was their target. On the other hand, I felt sorry for myself. Why couldn't I insult them back? I thought to myself. Looking over at my sister, I could tell she felt sorry for me as well. If anything, I should be standing up to them for her sake. I could not muster a single word. I grabbed my sister by the hand and went inside the house, feeling like a coward. I didn't tell anyone what had just happened. What is wrong with me? I pondered. I don't fit in with anyone. If only I were a White boy. At least Theodore Huxtable.

I was a great student in school, making good grades, and never getting into any trouble. I started to notice the little subtle differences among my classmates. Most of the Black kids, except for a few, including myself, were unruly. Not paying attention in class, talking out of turn, loud and disruptive. Most of the White kids, except for a few, raised their hands, were respectful, and participated in class. My young mind processed this as another example of my "whiteness" or my "blackness" depending on one's perspective. My perspective was conflicted. I looked no different from my Black counterparts; however, I talked and behaved like my White counterparts. Was there really that much of a difference or was it an illusion? I thought.

After school, my brother would watch my sister and I until my dad got home from work. Vick was my hero! Nine years older than me, there was nothing he did that I did not think was cool. My big brother introduced me to comic books; Vick had a whole box of them and would let me look through them from time to time. He promised them to me after he went away to college in the fall. His bedroom was the coolest place in our house by far. The walls of his room were covered with Prince and Bruce Lee posters. All types of cool knick-knacks and soon to be eighties memorabilia like rubik's cubes and boomerangs cluttered his desk alongside a Commodore 64 home computer, calculus, and French textbooks. Often enough, he would have his buddies come over. I studied them intensely, listening in on their conversations about girls, cars, and whatever else teenagers talked about. I remember thinking about how they had it made, and how I couldn't wait till I was in high school.

My brother would have his girlfriend come over too. Vivian and I both were delighted whenever she did come over. Vick was a lot nicer, and she treated us like her little brother and sister. One afternoon, Vick's girlfriend came over, and she and my brother disappeared into his bedroom. "She forgot to say hi, and he forgot our snacks." I told my sister, who was indulged in the television show we were watching. So, I went to remind them both of their forgetfulness. When I got to the door, I paused when I heard moans and the bedsprings squeaking from behind his closed door. What were they doing? I thought. Could they be jumping up and down on the bed? I had to see for myself. I entered the bedroom, and to my surprise, they weren't jumping up and down on the bed. They were half-naked, without any clothing on their lower bodies, sitting Indian style with their legs wrapped around one another.

The look on their faces was of sudden shock. I was speechless; I did, however, manage to wave at them both before my brother yelled, "What do you want?!" I stammered through asking for an apple, gawking at their entangled naked bodies. "Yes!" he shouted. "Get the apple! Just get out!" I closed the door confused about what I had walked in on. "Was that...sex?" I asked myself, walking to the kitchen. A smile contoured on my face. "I can't wait till I'm in high school." I declared, taking a bite of my apple.

The next day at school was the infamous picture day. Picture day for me was like being escorted to the gas chamber or the electric chair. My awkwardness, shyness, and whiteness were all on display for the entire school to see. I never smiled; a smirk or a grin was the best that I could do. My clothes were decent, clean, and nice-looking, thanks to my mom. My hair neatly trimmed, thanks to my dad. Neither my haircut nor my apparel would have me mistaken for a fashion model. They just weren't "in," at least not with the Black kids. My

OshKosh B'gosh didn't quite stand up to the 'oh so popular' Levi Strauss jeans, nor did my Pro-Keds to the Nike Cortez. My haircut was as plain as it could get, none of the funky fresh parts or designs that everyone else had. Not only did I talk and act White, but I also dressed White. I would think to myself as I waited in line to have my picture taken. "Be sure to smile." My mom would plead with me on picture day mornings. "You didn't last year." I could hear her voice in my mind, still pleading for a decent school picture of me as I sat down in front of the camera and the gray cloudy day backdrop. "Say cheese." the executioner would say. I have nothing to smile about, I thought, forcing a very robotic smile.

When I got off the school bus that day, Vick already had his friends over. They were practicing the lyrics and dance moves to ready for the world's "Tonight" for their high school talent show that winter. One of my brother's friends had brought along his niece, a half-Black, half-Filipino, eight-year-old girl named Cindy. I floated over to where she and my sisters sat playing with dolls. She had light olive skin, almond-shaped eyes, and long, sandy brown hair. I was in love! "Hey." I managed to say through my shyness. She smiled and said, "Hello!" After an hour or so went by of us playing "Teacher" and "Grocery Store" Cindy and I were an item. I could tell she liked me just as much as I liked her. What if she wants us to do the "Oochie Coochie"? I thought to myself as the three of us decided to play "House" next. The "Oochie Coochie" was in no way as sophisticated as what I walked in on my brother and his girlfriend doing. It was as simple as me lying on top of her humping, fully clothed, of course. I had got some practice with this at my cousin Junior's birthday party, where I was forced by him to do the "Oochie Coochie" with this very unpleasant, unattractive girl named Mookie. Between Mookie and Vivian's life-sized "walk with me" doll, I believed I was ready to play "House" with Cindy.

Just when I was about to ask her to be the Mama, she said, "Ok, you're the Daddy, and Vivian is our baby." "Ok!" I replied faster than a speeding bullet. After a few minutes of coaxing my sister into being an infant and going through the motions of feeding her and laying her down for an afternoon nap, Cindy grabbed my hand, and we went into our walk-in closet, turning off the lights and closing the door behind us. "It's time to go to bed." She said as she put down a blanket on the floor for us to lay on. Patting the vacant space next to her on the blanket, she said, "Lay down right here, honey, come to bed." My shyness was nowhere to be found; the butterflies that would usually flap about in my stomach in a manic frenzy, whenever I had to interact with another human being, were gone. I laid down beside her, and seconds later, I found myself on top of her, executing the perfect "Oochie Coochie" form. This was cut short by my sister/baby, turning on the lights, opening the door, and proceeding to ask for baby food. Cindy jumped up promptly. "Go to work, honey." She said, attending to the starving sister/baby as Cindy and her uncle prepared to leave home for the evening. I basked in the light of what she and I had done. On their way out the door, Cindy turned and kissed me on the cheek. Later, Vick had asked me what the kiss was all about? With a newfound attitude toward the opposite sex, I smiled and shrugged it off.

The Christmas of 1986 was a special one out of all the other Christmases up until that point. It was the only Christmas when my entire extended family got together to celebrate the holiday. My Grandmother Cara had twelve children. That's a lot of uncles, aunts, and cousins. It was magical to me.

My Grandmother Cara lived in the heart of the town, directly in the middle of the hood. When my mother would take us to visit her, she would always double-check to make sure she didn't leave anything of value in the seats or in sight and made sure that she locked all the car doors. Then she would rush my sister and I inside of the gate to close and lock it. My mother had a good reason for this paranoia.

"Uptown" was home to liquor houses that winos would congregate around, begging for loose change. By the mid-'80s, the crack epidemic had made its way to our small southern town like most places. However, the scariest thing there for me was the older uptown kids I would see at school and around the neighborhood. Still, there was an attraction to "uptown." It was dangerous, but it was ALIVE. Music from my uncle's club spiced the night air. The sound of women laughing, beer bottles breaking, loud profanity, and fighting was electric. One day, I'll be old enough to go there, I thought. Christmas cheer was everywhere; everyone seemed happy and festive, including me. At school, I became more vocal and started to make friends, both Black and White kids.

After school one day, my brother had to go back to his school to set up for the talent show he and his friends had spent weeks practicing for. He had our cousin Evon come over and watch us. She was cool as always and let us do anything we wanted. Evon would always tell me how she loved the color of my eyes and that I would be a ladies man when I grow up. I took it all in stride. She had to say things like that to her kid cousin, I thought.

After our afternoon snack and several episodes of our favorite cartoons, my sister would be fast asleep. I usually continued to watch television or headed outside to play. But that day, my cousin Evon had other plans. "Come here for a minute,." She said as loud as a whisper could be. She had just laid my sister down on her bed when I made it to the doorway. "Yes." I responded. "I need help with these." She said as she removed her sweater and bra, exposing her breast to me. I was dumbfounded and staring at her breast as she sat on my bed. As I approached, she quickly gathered me in her bosom, and I remained there until she was satisfied. When she was done with me and redressed in her bra and sweater, she reminded me not to tell anyone if we were to do this again. I promised not to tell a soul in fear of upsetting her, even though I did not feel bad about what happened. I thought about how her body felt for the next two days. Evon participated in the talent show as well. She sang Whitney Houston's "Greatest Love of All" and the crowd gave her a standing ovation. I felt like she was singing directly to me.

Chapter 2: Introduction To Racism

It had only been two years since my brother Vick had gone away to college. I had already made myself comfortable in his old room a week after he moved into his dorm room. By now, I had become more comfortable in my skin as well. The '90s were starting to look promising. My parents began giving me more freedom. I was allowed to grow my hair in a high-top and choose my clothes. Also, I received allowance for doing small chores around the house. The best part was having my bedtime extended to 11:00 p.m. or a little later to catch some of The Arsenio Hall Show, as they should have! I was now in junior high. My parents allowing me these privileges came nothing short of me having more responsibilities. I had piano lessons every Saturday morning and worked at his company throughout the week. Some weekends my mother would have me doing yard work or helping her out in her garden that felt like a plantation, even though it was maybe half an acre of land. Then there was church service on Sunday.

None of this helped out my social status. I decided to ask my parents if I could try out for the football team. It was entirely up to my mom; she agreed I could as long as it didn't interfere with anything. By the sixth grade, I had mastered the balance of making good grades and goofing off. This would allow me more time in between to chase girls. The summer of 1991 ending was just the beginning of the said chase. A nearby junior high school had closed its doors for good over the summer, so their student body combined with our student body and what bodies they were! Something had happened over the summer. My female counterparts had grown curves in places they did not have before school let out for the summer break. My friends and I could not keep our eyes or our hands, for that matter, to ourselves. We would cop a feel whenever the curves presented themselves. Sometimes we got a little extra.

Her name was Willow O'Conner, a cute White girl who had developed a lot over the summer. She stood 4'10", with a huge behind and chest. Willow sometimes would get and keep my attention by making her breast bounce. "Could I borrow a pencil?" she said flirtingly as her chest bounced slowly to a standstill. "Sure, you can have this one!" I'd reply as if I were none the wiser. Or if I were behind her in the hall, she would stop abruptly, causing me to crash into her pillow-like backside. "Sorry." She would say, running off giggling. After recess one day, a crowd of girls blindsided me. "Guess who likes you!?" their words buzzed in my ears like a swarm of bees. "I don't know...Who!?" I replied, surprised by all of the sudden attention. "Willow O'Conner." They said in unison. "You have to come right now." One of them said, while grabbing me and leading me over to where Willow was. As Willow and I locked eyes, a crowd began to form around us. If I didn't like Willow before today, I sure did now. We sheepishly greeted each other in the middle of the crowd, like two pugilists squaring off on pay per view. "Wanna kiss?" she asked. I smiled nervously and said yes. We wrapped our arms around each other, tilted our heads in the opposite directions, and pressed our lips against one another's. Then unexpectedly, she put her tongue into my mouth. The crowd let out this loud sitcom of a "Woooooooooo." I felt myself getting light-headed and her knees getting weak. The time seemed to stand still as we continued our exchange of tongues. "Teacher coming!" someone yelled from the crowd. We managed to pull ourselves apart as the crowd dispersed. Still in a daze from the kiss, Willow turned my hand over and wrote her phone number in my palm. "Call me tonight. OK?" she said, walking away blushing. I beamed at the thought of our kiss all day. The kiss wouldn't be the only unexpected attention I got that day. As I walked to the bus after the last school bell rang for the day, a group of girls once again blindsided me.

"Why were you kissing that White girl on break today?" one of them asked. "All these Black girls around and you couldn't find one to kiss?" another asked, obviously bothered. "Umm" was all I managed to say before they walked off, though not before one of them punched me in my shoulder, causing me to drop the books I held to scatter about the parking lot.

That night I talked to Willow on the phone for hours. We talked about the kiss, English class, and the class trip that was coming up. It went on like that for weeks, kissing at school and talking on the phone at home. That is until one night, I called, and Willow's dad answered the phone. "May I speak to Willow?" I asked politely. "Who's calling?" the curious voice asked. When I told him my name, there was this pregnant pause that followed. Willow isn't allowed to date no niggers!" Before hanging up the phone. Nigger...nigger, the word lingered around even after I had hung up the phone. It wasn't like I had never heard the word before. Nigger, I thought. Pictures of the Jim Crow era and slavery entered my mind as I turned the word over in my brain. I had never been called a "Nigger" by a White person to my face or in earshot before. So much for sounding White, I thought. At school, I noticed that Kenny Sutherland, the same blue-eyed, spiky blond-haired White boy I so much wanted to trade places with in elementary school, was now dressing like the Black kids, even using slang. How ironic! I thought. I was starting to like the idea of being a nigger.

Now that my brother was away in college, my Aunt Marcie would watch my sister and I until my dad got off of work. The projects became my happy place. With some other kids who lived there, my cousin Kaiden and I treated the place like we owned it. We were a gang of sorts, no more menacing than the little rascals. Every day was an adventure. If we weren't stealing plums from the neighboring houses, we were perfecting our acrobatic skills. Many days were spent walking on our hands, performing forward, backward and semi flips off the side of buildings and picnic tables. Often our excursions ended with us being chased by the police. They could never catch us after they gave chase inside of the projects. We were too fast and knew how to jump fences with ease, giving us enough time to scatter in several directions once we landed on the other side. Every day we had some mission.

This particular day we were joined by an older kid who lived uptown. He was visiting a relative. He was cool as a fan blade in the fall, commanding us without even trying. We all looked up to him. In his hand, he had this giant cup of red punch that he shared with us. Before passing the cup around he said, "Don't drink it fast, take sips." When it came around to me, I sniffed it first. "Just drink it!" he instructed, studying me. He then popped a cassette tape of N.W.A. in his boom box and then turned the volume way up. I took a swig of the concoction. It was Kool-Aid mixed with something a lot stronger.

Minutes later, we were all giddy, laughing, and carrying on. Some girls joined us that lived around the way. More of the red punch was poured and passed around, this time accompanied by cigarettes. The girls became as loose as we were, finding themselves to be too drunk to leave. They went from lap to lap, laughing and throwing up. I was having the time of my life. When the sun went down, we staggered our way back to my cousin's apartment. The older kid from uptown gave us his approval by giving us dap. "Y'all little niggas alright." He said before he disappeared out of our sight. Kaiden and I looked at one another, nodding our heads in agreement. Without having to say so, we knew we both had "street cred" now. By the time we made it back to his building, we could hear his mom calling for us. "Oh, shit."

My cousin said. "We late!" We reluctantly walked up the steps, and my Aunt Marcie's eyes were burning holes through us as we made it to the second floor. "Do y'all know what time it is?" she asked angrily. We said nothing. "Get inside and wash up for supper!" she said demandingly, with an open hand smacking the back of our heads as we entered the apartment.

My time in the projects was always exciting. I started picking up some bad habits though. One was stealing. It became so easy, so second nature; I became good at it. Mostly I would take candy from the corner stores or toys from the department stores. Not due to a lack of funds, I always had enough money to buy these things. It was the sheer adrenaline rush I would get from the pilfering.

Another habit I picked up was hustling. All the candy I lifted, I rarely ate myself. The Pixy Stix, Cow Tales, Lemonheads, and candy jewelry brought me a handsome return. I did well in the sugar-high trade until I was forced out by this heavyset girl whose mother worked at the candy packaging factory. She made me an offer I couldn't refuse. I turned my attention to a less threatening and more profitable market, comic books.

All those old comics my brother left me were a gold mine. I merged with another comic book pusher. We struck a 50/50 deal and went to work. Whenever the bell rang between classes, we opened up shop in the boy's bathroom, far from all the classrooms in the sixth-grade hall. Before the first bell rang in the morning and during lunch, we slang the polyurethane filled bags of superhero tales like dope, and like the dope game, we eventually got raided. The assistant principal hauled us into his office. It would be the first time I ever got into any trouble at school. I was petrified considering what my parents would say. My partner in crime and I sat in the principal's office for what seemed like an eternity. The principal came in, sat at his desk, and stared at both of us for a couple of seconds. "I'm not going to suspend you...this time." He said, looking over the rim of his glasses. We set up straight in our chairs. "What I am going to do is give you a paddling!" he retorted. He placed a foot-long wooden paddle on his desk. "Who's first?"

I walked back to class with a sore bottom and a note I had to take home to my parents to sign and return to the school the next day. When I entered the classroom, I tossed the letter into the trash can and took my seat. A note was passed up to me from the back of the classroom. I opened it reluctantly, and it read: "Do you like me? Check yes or no." Looking back in search of my admirer, I saw two girls smiling and waving at me. I checked yes and passed the note back to the sender, turning my attention finally back to the teacher.

Most Wednesdays, when my dad picked my sister and I up from my Aunt Marcie's, he would have picked up dinner from either Pizza Hut or Kentucky Fried Chicken. He barely ever changed the menu or the routine. Once home, he would put on an O'Jays' record as my sister, and I sat at the table for dinner. My dad was into being fit and working out, so after dinner, we would take a walk around the neighborhood, often ending up at my grandmother's and grandfather's house. One Wednesday, the routine of takeout, soul music, and walking was interrupted. My grandmother had slipped into a diabetic coma, my dad explained to my sister and I on our way to the hospital.

My Aunt Renee greeted us when we arrived at the hospital and said, "She's still in ICU, but she is stable." With a sigh of relief. My dad left us with her as he took the elevator up to see his mother. Shortly after, my Aunt Mimi and cousin Drake walked through the hospital entrance. He and I were the best of friends, even though we rarely got the chance to hang out as much as Kaiden and I did. My aunts talked among themselves. Drake and I walked away from the rest of my family. "My mom and I are moving to be closer to grandma and granddad in a couple of weeks." He said in an indifferent tone. That's good, I thought to myself. He cut short my daydream of us playing Nintendo all day when he said that our grandmother would have her leg taken off.

As the months passed and the school year came to an end, I managed to maintain my grades and stay out of trouble in school. Staying out of trouble at home was the problem. I dove into a pool of juvenile delinquency. I had finally got caught stealing. Greed and sloppiness got me caught with a pocketful of Transformer toys by an undercover security guard in a K-mart one beautiful Saturday while out shopping with my mom. She and the security were baffled as to why I would steal them when I had the money to buy them. Then I accidentally burned down our clubhouse. Boredom and a book of matches are bound to lead to a clubhouse fire. Oh, and then there was the school break-in that my gang from the projects did just for kicks. That resulted in some of us going to juvenile detention. I was one of the lucky ones, though I was punished severely! My mom and dad took turns in the onslaught of ass whoopings I received after each incident. I lost all privileges; going over to my cousin's house in the projects was the first to go. The telephone, Nintendo, and television were taken away as well. Also, no school dances and no football. My adolescent life was in ruins. All I had access to were encyclopedias and vocational Bible school that summer.

When the summer was over and the school year was about to begin, I had learned my lesson. I have to be more careful when I do shit, I thought. My parents sat down with me to discuss new responsibilities for the new school year. They both felt I was old enough to stay home without any adult supervision after school. They also agreed that I could start playing football again. I was overwhelmed with thoughts of the up and coming school year. "Thanks, Mom. Dad, I won't let you down." I promised them while hugging their necks collectively. During the following weeks, I spent most of my time on the telephone trying to catch up and see what I had missed out on over the summer. Drake had moved into our grandparent's house, so he hadn't missed any of the action that summer. He filled me in, appropriately: The older kids from uptown had terrorized everyone else in the town by putting them in the "scissors" wrestling move, causing the victim to shit on themselves. The one girl I was crushing on during the school year moved on after she didn't hear from me during my punishment. He told me she got "fingered" by some kid from our class at the dance. I wasn't going to let the seventh grade pass me by, I thought as my cousin continued to fill me in.

In preparation for the first day of seventh grade, which might as well have been the preparation for my presidency, I went through my checklist. Haircut checked, outfit checked, sneakers checked. I placed my ensemble on the chair in the living room: a Black Bart Simpson doing the signature Michael Jordan dunk T-shirt lay over a pair of Karl Kani shorts, a pair of Air Jordan's sat underneath it all. I hopped down and did ten push-ups before flexing in the mirror. I was ready! That morning I rushed through breakfast, got dressed, and went to the bus stop. My neighbor and homeboy, Thurgood, was already waiting for the high school bus. "Yo, you leaving us kids this school year, huh?" I teased him as I extended my hand for our exclusive handshake. "Yea, man. I'm in the major league now." He said, laughing at our conversation. "Where were you this summer?" I asked, eyeballing his outfit from head to toe. "New Jersey." He said with a grin. As the bus stop started to get crowded, we finished our "rooster strut" by doing the "Kid 'n Play" dance, brushing off our shoes immediately afterward. His bus came, and we shook hands again before he boarded the bus.

By the time I made it to my school, the place was swarming with pre-teens with new clothes, haircuts, and hairdos. Making my way through the crowd, I found Drake already posted up in the seventh-grade hall by the lockers, talking to every girl that passed by. "Yo, over here!" he shouted. I made my way to where he and the other guys from our class had posted up, gawking at the female student body. This is going to be a great year, I thought. In my first class, I had to try extra hard to concentrate on what the teacher was saying. All the girls were in a hissy about something, and it continued down the hall after class. What were they talking about? I wondered. Not now. I am finally focused. I have to find Casey.

Casey and I met the previous summer through our mothers, who went to high school with one another. She was fine as all on the outside, with long silky hair, smooth caramel skin, and some huge breasts. She was transferred to our school that year, so I had to get to her before the other guys had the chance to dig their claws into her. When I did find Casey, she was with some other girls. I made my move by sliding between her and her crew. "Hey, Casey, looking cute today!" "Thanks." She said, batting her eyes. We chatted for a while as I tried to focus on what she was saying instead of how she looked. Her next words broke my concentration. "Hey, could you do me a favor and introduce me to the new kid from Connecticut?" What!? I thought. Then it all came together for me. All the whispers, all the chit chat between the girls in the hall and in class, was about some new nigga from Connecticut. I walked away from Casey and her crew without giving her an answer. "Who is this guy?" I asked several confidants. No one seemed to know exactly. At recess, everyone had made their way to the front of the seventh-grade building. Once a flipping contest started, I noticed the new kid who wooed all the girls in the seventh grade. He didn't look like much: light skin complexion, tight high top fades, a single earring piercing, his clothes were on point. That was about it, I thought as I sized him up. He took off in a sprint as I continued my hating from the sidelines. My eyes followed his accession.

Cartwheel, backward, backward, semi backward. Not bad, I thought, untying my shoes, getting in line for my turn to shine, thinking of the perfect combination I could use to top this. As the line of street acrobats moved on, I scanned the crowd for Casey. Upon spotting her, I took off in a sprint. Forward, forward, no hand forward. It was on! The gauntlet had been thrown down. As the flipping competition went on, I found myself behind my archnemesis in line. "Nice semi you got there, dude." I said sparingly. "Thanks!" He replied proudly. "My name is Kaiden." Before he finished his next sentence, the bell to end recess rang, then we all went to our next period classes.

When I made it to my next period class, I found he was also in it. "Great." I said under my breath and proceeded to my desk. When the teacher called the rollcall and got to my name, I yelled out, "present." The new kid was sitting right beside me. When the teacher called his name, he raised his hand and turned to me and gave a head nod. Being that he was sitting right by my side, I couldn't help but notice his notebooks. He had used the eraser to erase color to design graffiti. I had done the same with my notebooks, so I thought it was pretty cool that we had that in common. He noticed my artwork too. We gave each other the nod of approval. This guy might be cool after all, I convinced myself during the rest of the period. As we walked out of the class after the period ended, Kaiden leaned in and asked me if I "rhymed?"

Kaiden and I became really cool with each other. Inseparable, in fact, after that day. He lost the battle of Casey's affection to me, but he didn't suffer from the loss. Plenty of other girls desired him, so she was lost in the shuffle. By now, I had a full schedule, football practice, chores, piano lessons, and socializing. Fall and winter had passed before I knew it. Everything was going as I had hoped.

Chapter 3: The Grim Reaper

The spring of 1991 was in full swing. What better time is there to teach pre-teens about the birds and the bees. We had to register and get permission from our parents to attend the sex education class. I made sure to turn my permission slip in ahead of time. I feel most of the guys, including myself, thought sex-ed would be a co-ed experience and that the discussion of sex would have our female counterparts hot and bothered, and would then start "putting out." To say we were disappointed is an understatement. The class was too technical. We might as well had been trying to build a vagina rather than getting inside one. I did, however, learn about masturbation. I couldn't believe what I was hearing. I could have sex with myself?!?

The seventh grade proved to be the year of living for me. Then I was introduced to the Grim Reaper. Arriving at school that day, I was unaware of what had happened the night before. It didn't take long to see something irreversible had taken place. The entire student body was in a somber mood, almost silent as they went about their morning. I went to my usual morning hangout in front of the lockers in the seventh-grade hall, looking for the crew, but they weren't there. As I made my way around the school campus, I noticed some students were crying, and others were consoling them. Ok, this is weird, I thought. Finally, I found Kaiden in the cafeteria. He had his face in hands, sobbing while a teacher patted him on the back. I froze like a deer in headlights. She looked at me shaking her head. Simultaneously, an announcement came over the PA system. As a result of last night's unfortunate events, we will be honoring the lives lost of the two exceptional high school students. We will be offering to counsel anyone who feels they can benefit." Time stood still for me after hearing the principal's message. One of the high school students that died the previous night was Kaiden's cousin. They were close, and Kaiden looked up to him. I was told that the two students had been killed in a car accident after leaving their basketball game.

In my own family, my Aunt Candace was on her deathbed. I was one of the only people in the close family who didn't go see her yet. I didn't know the severity of the situation, nor did I want to go to the hospital. My mom told me Aunt Candace had requested to see me, so I gathered the courage to go. We walked into my aunt's hospital room. The sound of a breathing machine and other peeps and pings gave the place a sterile vibe that creeped me out right away. On the drive over to the hospital, I asked my mom what my aunts' illness was. "Cirrhosis of the liver." She said morbidly. I assumed my Aunt Candace would be her usual bright-eyed, bushy-tailed self when I turned to greet her in the hospital room. I got the full realization that my Aunt Candace, who had found some amusement in pinching her nephews and nieces, who was always the life of the party and who kept a beer can or a red cup in her hand, was dying.

As she laid there sleeping with the full capacity of tubes her body could withhold, I couldn't take my eyes off of her. I found myself not being able to move past the foot of her bed. My mother softly shook her sister, arousing her from her slumber. "Hey, Candace." She said with her voice cracking as she tried to keep it together, "I brought someone to see you." My aunt opened her eyes and sat up. I tried to hide my discomfort.

She had lost so much weight and was practically skin and bones. The pupils of her eyes were no longer white and had become yellow in hue. In a pleasant tone she said, "Hey, nephew. Come give your favorite aunty a hug." I did as she asked, once again trying to mask my discomfort. She then went into scolding me about all the trouble I got into last year.

"And don't think I don't know you been sipping." By "sipping." She meant drinking hard liquor. "You might think drinking is cool cause your friends doing it." Her voice was getting louder with each word. "Well, it's not cool! You don't won't to end up like me, now do you, boy?" I was fighting back tears, and so was she. "No, ma'am." I finally managed to say. She tried speaking again but had worked up a cough. "Go get your aunt a soda from the nurse." My mother said intervening. I was more than glad to leave the room. What an awful thing to happen to Aunt Candace, I thought as I walked to the nurses' station.

On the way home from the hospital, my heart was heavy. As I looked out the passenger seat window, I pondered: Why do people have to die? Where was God when the two high school students were killed in the car accident? Why was my Aunt Candace's last days alive filled with such pain and suffering? What does that mean for me? How would I die?

A couple of months had passed since my final goodbye to my Aunt Candace had occurred. One morning as my sister and I were having breakfast before school, I studied my father, who was unusually quiet, staring out of the kitchen window. He turned to us and said, "I need to talk to you guys about what happened last night." He said dreadfully, moving to the table where we sat. "Your cousin Tyler was killed in a drive-by last night." His words tapered off. My sister dropped her spoon in shock. "But he was just a kid!?" she said before bursting into tears. I continued to look at my breakfast. My dad placed his hand on my sister's shoulder as she sobbed. "You can stay home from school today if you choose." He said with concern. My mind went into overdrive, once again trying to figure out death.

My cousin Tyler had been in the wrong place at the wrong time. He was an incredibly smart kid for the age of ten. Smart, both academically and streetwise, he had ventured uptown to find his brother to talk him out of twenty dollars from his hustling stash. Some threatening words were exchanged between the older guys on the block and some out of towners earlier in the day. When the gang from out of town returned, Tyler had just met with his brother and was on his way back home as the out of towners drove up the block and spotted the guys that had forced them off the neighborhood earlier. An AK 47 appeared out of the car's passenger side as it slowed down just yards away from Tyler. Shots rang out as people began to scream and scatter, running in fear of their lives, taking cover as the car sped away down the street. The intended victim was able to reach shelter and return fire as the vehicle sped away around the corner, only to notice the pool of blood that Tyler lay engulfed in on the sidewalk. Three of the sixteen shots fired had entered his innocent body. One of the bullets went through his neck, severing his spine and ricocheting out the back of his head. The second had taken off his index finger on his left hand. The third went through his left hip bone and severed his penis from his body.

Whereas I had not been to a funeral in the past, it had only been six months since I attended my first, and now, I was at a third one. At each one, I could feel the sadness that lay on the mourning like a fog in spring, but I never cried. Not one single tear dropped from my eyes. Even though I could empathize with the grief, I had none of my own. Where was all this emotion and sadness and hurt going? I wondered. I often thought of my mortality. Surely everyone must die. What is the point of living, or being kind and doing your best if we are doomed to meet the Grim Reaper, who goes about picking people to join him as a florist would go about choosing flowers for a flower arrangement?

Things started to get back to normal as the days turned into weeks, and weeks turned into months. Ever since Tyler's funeral, though, I had changed. A switch had been flipped, turning off all hopes and dreams of living to old age. Previously, I was cool, calm, and collected. Now those emotions had been replaced with a burning rage, and the flames would reach up, right beneath the surface. At school, I got into a fight with Kenny Sutherland. He had overthrown a baseball pitch, and it struck me, bruising my ego more than it did me any physical harm. Another fight ensued with a friend of mine that had tried to finger a girl I was sweet on. They were considerable violations, but in the past, I would have brushed them off.

Now with any violation that came my way, my outlook on life was to dust them off with my fist. Subconsciously, I showed the Grim Reaper that I was a fighter and that he couldn't and shouldn't take me like he took the people of the funerals I had attended. His only chance of plucking me would be when I'd be old and no longer able to put up a fight. Even then, I would put him to the task. My parents and teachers grew concerned with this newfound outlet of mine. They offered advice and help, which I refused. Also, I would refute their concerns. "At least my grades are still good." I would say passively.

Chapter 4: Attention

Summer was right around the corner; I did my best to hold off any other disruptive episodes to avoid jeopardizing my summer like I had done the previous summer. I finished the school year in high fashion with no other fights and a 3.5 GPA. The summer ushered in all-around chaos for my hometown. It succumbed to an all-out war with a neighboring rival town. There were constant sounds of shooting coming from uptown. The police patrolled day and night, stopping any and every one that looked out of place. It wasn't safe to be outside during this time. I would walk the streets of uptown, passing by the blood-stained concrete where my little cousin was slain. I felt invincible out there. Sometimes saying out loud, "Come on motherfucker"—a catcall for the Grim Reaper that went unnoticed. Other kids weren't so fortunate. So many stories of kids being beaten up and jumped or shot at by the out of towners had come back to me. I was unbothered by them all.

One day, I found myself in the middle of one of the battles. "Watch out!" someone yelled, running as fast as they could toward me. I couldn't recognize if the guy was from uptown or out of town. Suddenly, I heard people shouting from behind him, giving chase. "Stop that Nigga!" One of the voices said from the mob. I realized then that the guy headed directly toward me was an out of towner who had been separated from his mob. He was right up on me before I knew it. I had to do something, so I stuck out my foot to trip the assailant. He was running so fast that when my foot connected with his shin, it sent him flying mid-air, and he landed with a thud to the ground with the wind knocked out of his lungs. The mob that was after him made their way to where he lay, and I stood by now. They proceeded to stump and punch the out of towner as he pleaded for them to stop. One of them recognized me. "Nice punch, cuz! Go home now. It's not safe to be out here right now." he said, impressed and concerned. I recognized him as well. It was the older kid that used to get me tipsy during my days of running around in the projects. I turned around and darted off to my house. Did he say, "nice punch?" I asked myself, panting as I made it to my front yard.

The next day Drake come over to my house to hang out. Word of my punch had traveled quickly. I decided not to tell people I had only tripped him down since it made me sound like such a badass. Besides, it was a real badass that was going around saying it, not me. "Everybody talking about how you knocked the dude out!" Drake said proudly. I quickly changed the subject. "Yea, hey what's up with the dance Friday night? Sneakers or Slacks?" That meant whether the party was being given by an older person or a younger person, describing the dress code needed to attend. "Sneakers." he said, grinning like a Cheshire cat. We had some serious planning to do. A "sneaker party" was when someone slightly older, yet cooler adult was hosting the event, which meant they would let us do whatever the hell we wanted. We made sure to invite all the new girls that transferred to our school that year and the girls from other schools that we had met at football and basketball games. The girls that we knew since we started school were sure to come anyway. The idea was to make the ratio of girls to guys 3:1. Showing the new girls more attention than the girls we had known for years and turning around and giving the other girls from other schools all of our attention, by the end of the night would ensure that we would end up with a phone number or two, or what we really wanted, which was to get laid.

At this party, I had planned to rock the mic for the first time. Kaiden and I would trade rhymes at school during lunch that would draw in a crowd. We had become known for rapping our asses off by the time the school year ended. The party would be our chance to shine, with a DJ, stage, and a larger crowd. I called Kaiden up immediately and gave him the detail. He agreed and said he would start writing his rhyme right away. We were almost set with our preparation for the dance that Friday. The only thing left to do was to get a "Brewer Brothers" haircut. The Brewer brothers were much older guys from our neighborhood who were responsible for our back to school picture day, and dance hair transformations. They would perform this ballad of duel haircutting on their mother's back porch and would charge those of us in school only five dollars for the craftsmanship. Like any other barbershop, there was a lot of shit talking that took place. Anything and everything were up for discussion while at their pop-up barbershop. We mostly got teased for still being virgins and peer pressured into taking a hit of a joint or taking a shot of liquor. Still, it was a safe and brotherly environment. Either Brewer brother cut my hair perfectly. Shortly after I got in the chair they would ask me about my brother Vick, whom they went to school with. They would give my brother his just due and mention how he and I were so different, like night and day. At first, it would bother me a little. Vick was my hero, but as I got older and the more I heard the comparison, the more I liked hearing it. Drake and I left the Brewer Brothers with fresh new haircuts and a fading buzz. He and I went separate ways, agreeing to meet up once we were dressed to drink up the gin he would take from our grandfather's sock drawer. I went home, ate, showered, and dressed, hyped about that night's dance. On my way over to meet Drake, I went over my rhymes in my head. This is going to be a night to remember, I thought to myself.

Everything about that night was magical. As we stepped into the party, gladly handing over our ten dollars for admission, DJ Kool's "The Water Dance" was blaring from the enormous speakers. The party was in full swing. We had made sure to show up fashionably late, making sure the community center building was packed to capacity. It was. Walking through the sea of party people, it seemed I was greeted with a smiling face, and every hand extended for me to dap. We made our way over to the speakers to get the best view of the dance floor. Secretly, I wanted to see the records that the DJ had. On the dance floor, there were plenty of girls already dancing, giggling, and sweating out their new hairdos. I looked over to the side where people were sitting, searching for a fresh, non-sweaty dance partner. "I'll be back." I shouted over the loud music to Drake. He nodded in agreement. Squeezing through the crowd, I tried not to cut through the couples in the darkest parts of the community center, knowing what I would be doing in the darkness. I wanted to be considerate of the guy that finally got his hands down some girl's pants. I made my way to the annex, and just as I was about to pay for a soda, I saw her. She was gorgeous! Dark mahogany skin, big brown eyes, and a big ole butt! Who was this? I asked myself, scrolling through my mental Rolodex. "Dammmmn" is what actually came out of my mouth. She smiled and disappeared into the girls' bathroom with the rest of her crew in tow. At that moment, the DJ started playing Father MC's "I'll Do 4 U." I broke my neck trying to get back to the dance floor. With a cup in hand, I slid on to the dance floor, dancing by myself at first until a girl took the bait and joined me. All night long, I alternated between dancing with a girl and hanging out with my homies, going outside for fresh air, and going to the annex for a soda. Inadvertently, I was looking out for the brown-eyed girl with the big butt. I ran into Kaiden finally, and he told me the DJ was ready for us. The brown-eyed girl would have to wait.

There is no better way to describe getting up on a stage for the first time than comparing it to a beautiful nightmare. With sweaty palms, stomach in knots, mouth dry with all eyes on me, I held the microphone with one hand and the other hand behind my back. I scanned the crowd for one person to concentrate on. There she was again, the brown-eyed girl. I smiled on the inside, keeping the look of cool on the outside. I leaned over to the DJ. "Hey, do you have the DWYCK instrumental?" He nodded, knowing that the Gang Starr record was one of the dopest out at the time. As he cued the record up, I took front stage and warmed the crowd up with: "Yo, party people; I need all the ugly people in the crowd to be quiet!" I said sarcastically. The crowd went bananas yelling and beating on things. I proceeded to shout out the neighborhoods in our town. The DJ gave me a scratch to let me know when to start rapping. My mind then went into autopilot, reciting the rhyme I had just wrote days before. Two minutes later, I came out of my trance to a cheering crowd of my peers. I passed the microphone off to Kaiden. "You killed it!" he said beamingly. "Get 'em!" I told him as I dapped him up and left the stage. He proceeded, in the same manner, hyping up the already hyper crowd. When the rap cypher came to an end, the DJ announced the last song of the night and dropped the needle on "If I Ever Fall in Love" by Shai. I looked up, recognizing the weight of such a song on the crowd of teens and pre-teens. The brown-eyed girl came over and asked if I wanted to dance with her. "Why not!" I replied with a smile. In my mind, we were the only two people left in the building, and this was our song. She placed her arms around my neck as I wrapped my arms around her waist, interlocking my hands. "What's your name?" I asked softly in her ear. "Keyva." she looked at me and said. "I already know yours." She said with a giggle. I let my hands find their way to her voluptuous behind, pulling her closer to me and palming her backside like Michael Jordan would palm a basketball. Without missing a beat, she removed my hands and placed them back on her waist. We exchanged numbers after the dance, and I promised to give her the next day. I walked home alone as I wanted to reflect on the nights' events.

As I looked up at the night sky, I never took the time to notice it before, but it was perfect. Everything in its proper place, working in unison just like tonight at the dance. Maybe, just maybe, the Grim Reaper had figured out he had best leave this one alone for the time being.

The rest of the summer was pale in comparison to how the summer had started. The war between my town and the out of towners was over with few casualties. It was safe again to be out during the day, and the community as a whole took advantage of it. My homie Thurgood and I went to the summer camp to kill time during the day. I had instantly become friends with this White kid named Matthew. It had been a long time since I had met someone with similar interests in things other than clothes, girls, sports, etc. As the summer camp came to an end, we exchanged numbers to stay in touch until school started back. The last day of summer camp was a free day, so everyone was in the gymnasium, running around, doing different activities. Matthew and I decided to practice shooting three-pointers at the basketball goal. One of his shots had bricked against the rim and with the force of a cannonball, hit this Black kid in the back of the head. When Matthew went over to retrieve the ball and apologize, the Black kid chucked the ball so hard at him that it hit him square in the chest. It sent Matthew falling to the gym floor. I ran over to Matthew. "Hey, are you ok, man?" Before he could answer, I turned around and pushed the Black kid as hard as I could. "What the hell, man, he didn't mean it!" I yelled, which got the attention of the teachers. As the Black kid stepped toward me, Thurgood stepped in between us. "Yo, don't fight here, wait till after camp is over and do this behind the building." The Black kid and I looked at each other and agreed.

Just like in the old Western movies, the showdown was to be at high noon. When the camp was over, everyone had heard about the fight and were all waiting behind the school gymnasium for us to show. "He's not gonna show." Someone yelled from the crowd as a couple of minutes had gone by. "What a gip!" one girl said, leaving in disappointment. The more time that passed the more confident I became. The fact was I hadn't lost a fight at that point anyway. That and the exaggerated story of my "one hit knock punch" must have scared the kid off I thought. The crowd dispersed, disappointed they had not seen a fight. Matthew shook my hand vigorously. "Thanks for taking up for me, man, see you in eighth grade." He said, satisfied there wasn't a fight on his behalf. Thurgood and I walked home in triumph. It was a win by default, but still a win for our neighborhood.

About 3:30 that afternoon, my doorbell rang, and it was Thurgood. "Yo, that kid from camp wants to talk to you." He said passively. "Ight, let me grab my shoes." I walked outside to meet the kid and Thurgood, where they stood waiting for me to come out. "No show today. What gives?" I asked the kid as I approached them. "Something came up." He said reluctantly. "Yea, well let's squash all this ..."

Before I could complete my sentence, the kid had thrown a wicked right hook, landing square on my upper lip. I hit the ground grabbing my face in shock from the blow. "Yo, that's fucked!" Thurgood said to the kid as he spotted a pair of brass knuckles on his fist. "Dude, you ok?" he asked frantically. I could taste blood through the numbness of my lip. Without responding, I watched the kid hop on his bike and peddle off. Thurgood helped me to my feet. "Damn, man, let me see your face? That pussy hit you with brass knuckles, man, your lip is split and swollen." I couldn't say anything. It felt as if my lip was going to fall off my face if I tried to use them. I had to see this for myself. "I gotta go home." I said, managing to speak through my tightened lips.

Once inside the house, Thurgood had made a cold compress to stop the bleeding and swelling. "Here, put this right on the cut." He said, handing me the compress. "Let me see." I pleaded. "No, let the swelling go down." He rebutted. "Fuck that!" I said, making my way to the bathroom mirror. I removed the compress to reveal a bloody, swollen mess of an upper lip. "I'll kill 'em!" I said wholeheartedly, dashing out of the bathroom into the living room where Thurgood and my sister Vivian were. "He wanna use weapons to fight?" I asked rhetorically, scanning the house for something I could grab. My eyes focused on the perfect weapon, my dad's bullwhip. I rolled it up into a coil and headed for the door with Vivian and Thurgood hot on my heels.

They tried to stop me from going over to the kid's neighborhood in fear I would get jumped or worse. I didn't listen to their pleas. I couldn't listen. All I could see was the color red and this kid's face. I hopped on my bike and headed over to his neighborhood; the problem was I didn't know which house he lived in, so I rode around the neighborhood, speculating which house was his. The more I searched, the angrier I got. Then it dawned on me. I was classmates with someone that lived over here. A real stand-up guy. He would know which house this kid lived in and would tell me, even if it meant giving up one of his own. I peddled faster until I reached my classmate's home. He was already outside with other kids from their neighborhood. They looked as if they had seen a ghost as I pulled up into the carport. "Where is he?" I asked my classmate. "Yo, man, please don't start a fight here, my mom will be here any minute." he said beggingly. Just then, the kid that had sucker punched me came out of my classmate's house with a smug look on his face until he saw me standing there. "Come out in the street." I said calmly, even though I could feel my temperance fleeting. I made the offer only not wanting to get my friend in trouble with his mom. Otherwise, I would have laid into this kid with the whip by now. I waited until he came off of the steps before reaching for the whip I had tucked away in my shorts. When the whip was in sight, the rest of them jumped to their feet in fear. The last thing anyone expected to see was a Black kid using a whip on another Black kid in a fight. I whipped it a couple of times to show I knew how to use it. "Clickcaw, clickcaw." The whip sliced the air like little lightning strikes during a thunderstorm. The kid pleaded with me not to hit him with the whip. I wasn't backing down. I could smell the fear from all of them. He tried to make a run for the door. "Clickcaw, clickcaw." I cracked the whip between him and his escape route. He pleaded more as his friends looked around not saying a word. He managed to grab a nearby yard rake to try to defend himself. I snapped the whip again, making the tail wrap around the handle of the rake, then yanking it with all my might to pull it loose from his grip. By this time, Thurgood had pulled up on his bike. I could hear him calling me from the street. As I cornered the kid, the look of fear and regret in his eyes began to calm me. I turned away without giving him the lashes I wanted to leave him with so badly. What I did leave him with was better than I could have imagined. I left him with respect for me out of fear. I hopped on my bike, and Thurgood and I began to make our way back home. "Damn, Indiana Jones, you feel better now?" he said, trying to lighten the mood. "Yea, I do." I said as the rage inside of me subsided. We rode off into the sunset back to our side of the town.

Chapter 5: Too Black?

"Hello, may I speak to Rodney?" a young female asked when I answered the phone. My left eyebrow raised in curiosity. "Umm, you have the wrong number, but who needs Rodney when you can have me." I replied slyly. When she giggled at my statement, I knew I had her. I had heard of this type of situation happening before. My homies had told me they would receive this random phone call where a girl was trying to contact some other dude, and it turned out to be a "freak" on the other end of the phone. I was still a virgin, technically. I mean, I had finger banged a couple of girls, but it was not "The Real Deal" Holyfield. So, when this opportunity presented itself that day, I was more than eager to see just how far it would go. We formally exchanged names and numbers. Her name was Sharon, and I could tell by the suffix in the phone number that she was from the rival town that my town stayed beefing with at the beginning of the summer. I weighed my options.

Sure death by the hands of the out of towners or starting the eighth grade or even high school still a virgin? I decided to take my chance with the out of towners. "Hello, you still there?" she asked, interrupting my thought on the matter. "Yes, give me your address, and I'll give you mine so we can send each other pictures." She said ok and proceeded to provide me with her information. I hung up the phone with her, thinking about how good looking she sounded over the phone. A couple of days passed since I had mailed off my picture and letter to Sharon.

We talked every day on the phone. She took precedence over all the other girls I was talking to at the time. She told me she finally got my letter and loved it and how fine I looked in the picture. Not to mention all the things she said she would do to me once we were face to face. So as can be imagined, I was anxious to get her picture and letter.

After harassing my mother day in and day out about checking the mail, one day she finally said, "Who is Sharon?" Holding back laughter as she flashed the letter in front of me. "Nobody!" I exclaimed, snatching the letter from her and walking as fast as I could to my bedroom. I ripped open the envelope trying to get to the picture of the girl that would unknowingly be taking my virginity. I stared at the picture for a moment. She looks...ok, I guess, I thought, highly disappointed. Not at all what I was used to. Sharon, on a scale of 1–10, peaked at a 5. I called her and told her I had received her letter, pretending to be just as excited as she was.

Virgins can't be choosey, I thought. We made plans for her to come over the next day. I spent the early part of the day cleaning and picking my room. I know I must have read her letter with all the freaky little details she included in it a hundred times. I need to get motivated; this is it! I thought. I'm about to have sex right here, on this bed today! I said, getting excited at the thought. I hopped up on the mattress and gave a few quick humps. The day went on, and no call came from Sharon. Don't worry, I said to myself, I only talk to her after 4:00 p.m. anyways. Why would today be any different? The afternoon had turned into night. My dad returned home from work, and shortly after that, we had dinner. That's when I finally admitted to myself that I got stood up.

The time was now eight o'clock. At that moment, the doorbell rang, and my dad went to answer it. I listened with a careful ear from the kitchen. It was Sharon; she had made it after all. My dad called for me to greet my company. I took some time to come out, to gather my composure, then walked into the living room. "Hey Sharon, you made it!" I said, trying to hide my excitement. She looked a lot better in person, I thought as I greeted her with a hug. I got an instant erection when our bodies touched. "Sorry I'm so late. My ride backed out on me, and I had to catch a cab." "A cab!?" my dad and I said in unison. "Ok then." I said, stalling my dad from asking the questions we both were thinking. Did she think she was staying over? And how was she getting back home? "Follow me." I said while grabbing her hand and whisking her away to my bedroom. "Keep the door open back there!" my dad shouted. This was not going as I had planned, but I was going to make the best of it. Now that we were alone, I gave Sharon another look over. Her hair was done up in braids, and this hairstyle made her look older than she was. She stood about 4'5"; her breasts made her look her age. I felt a little better after examining her and took a seat in my game chair as she took a seat on my bed. "Would you like something to drink?" I asked. She laughed and said, "Yes, you talk so white. I love talking to you." She smiled, and I returned with a grin. As I walked to the kitchen to retrieve the drinks, I made sure to observe whether or not my dad was on his way to bed. If he wasn't going to sleep, my chances of sex were slim to none.

He was still up and gave me a look that said, what is going on right now. I returned the gaze with a shrug. A half-hour had passed; my dad had made several security sweeps back to the bedroom to check on my company and me before finally going to bed, but not before telling me that Sharon needed to leave no later than ten o'clock. It was now nine o'clock, time was of the essence. Sharon had chewed at least five sticks of Big Red gum by now. My room reeked of hot cinnamon. I figured she was just nervous. Up until my dad retired to his bedroom, we just talked about nothing in particular, really just buying time. We both knew what she came over for. Now that he was done patrolling, it was time to get to it.

Without warning, Sharon made her move. "Let me see it?" she said playfully. I knew what "It" Sharon was referring to. I stood up and walked in front of her, where she sat on the bed. I pulled my semi-firm penis out and she smiled with delight. As she took me into her hand, she began stroking me, staring at my face then back at my penis as it grew in thickness and length. I was harder than a roll of quarters. "You think you are going to put all this in me?" she asked teasingly. I stood there with my pants and boxers around my ankles, not saying a word.

What eventually came out was, "We can't do this here; my dad may come back here." Sharon then motioned to my walk-in closet. "In there?" she asked. Why hadn't I thought of that, I thought as I grabbed her hand. "Yes, in there; let's go!" "Ok!" she giggled as she popped yet another stick of gum into her mouth as she got up from the bed. I walked my way to the closet first with my dick in my hand, and my pants still around my ankles. Upon entering, I thought about how we would pull it off; there was so much crap on the closet floor.

When I turned around, Sharon was on her knees. Before I could say anything, she grabbed my dick again. Except this time putting my member into her mouth. My left eyebrow raised from the hot wetness of her mouth that made the nerve endings in my dick surge. She allowed my shaft to penetrate her throat before gagging and taking it out again. I could feel myself starting to stand on the tip of my toes. I tried to speak but couldn't; she was now slobbering and sucking faster and faster, using her hands to massage the shaft and head of my penis, all while staring up at me. She squeezed my swollen flesh as I began to thrust it into her mouth.

I could feel my load traveling from my loins until it reached the tip of my penis. "Mmmm hmm." She said, still sucking on me as I exploded into her mouth. I killed over from the sensation. "Holy shit!" I said, looking at her in awe. She stood up and wiped her mouth. "Did you like it?" "Hell, yea!" I replied, trying to catch my breath. "Good." she said with achievement in her tone as she came in for a kiss. I stopped her dead in her tracks. "Umm, let me see what time it is." I said sternly. I pulled up my boxers and pants and walked into the bathroom. My legs were shaking as I stumbled along the way.

I looked at myself in the mirror and laughed out loud but quietly. Yo, that shit felt so good! I looked at the clock; it was 9:30 p.m. I walked back into the bedroom and took a seat next to her on my bed. I put my hand between her legs and rubbed her crotch before I started to unzip her zipper. "I wouldn't do that if I were you." She said in a sing-song way. "Oh, why is that?" I asked. "My period came down yesterday." She said sheepishly. I snatched my hand back in disgust. "I'm sorry. I know you wanted to..." "It's ok." I said, interrupting. "It's getting late anyway. We can have sex the next time." I was lying. This would be the last time I made an effort to speak or see Sharon again. "Ok." she said, thankfully wrapping her arms around my neck. "Let me use your phone so that I can call the cab." As I handed her the phone, I couldn't help but feel sorry for Sharon. I was appreciative of the blow job. I couldn't help but think how many other guys she had been with in this way, and who the hell was Rodney? "Cabbie said he would be here in fifteen minutes." She said, turning to me as she hung up the phone. Good, I thought. She will be out of here soon enough. I unzipped my pants and motioned for her to come to me. She quickly obliged and dropped to her knees between my legs.

The summer had dwindled to its last day. By now, all my school shopping had been completed. I went through my usual checklist of back-to-school freshness. I was well on my way to the eighth grade, my last year of junior high school. Although I was still technically a virgin, it didn't matter. That blow job from Sharon would make for great conversation with my homies. As I lay in the bed, staring at the ceiling, I practiced my freestyle rhyming until a thought hit me like a ton of bricks. The eighth-grade homecoming court, I thought. This would secure my status of being one of the cool kids forever. I fell asleep thinking about becoming one of the junior high's royalty. That year would prove to be one of the best school years ever.

On the first day of school, we started what would be a tradition for years to come. My closest friends and I would smoke a joint and sip liquor before the bus arrived at our bus stop. I think I tried to date every girl in the eighth grade. I'm sure I had set a record for the shortest relationship in eighth-grade history with this girl named Tameka. It would only last from the beginning of our first break to the end of the 6th period. She kicked me in the balls and said that I acted too Black to be her boyfriend. The irony of it all is that she was Black as well. All my achievements weren't foolishness. I had joined the band and learned to play the alto saxophone, adding to my musical prowess. I was accepted into the F.B.L.A. (Future Business Leaders of America) and was moved into A.G. (Academically Gifted) English class. I worked my butt off. I was performing a perfect balance of being a social misfit and an academic statesman. The work ethic would pay off. I was elected vice president of the entire eighth grade, a superficial title at best. The cherry on top of the oh so sweet year was the Homecoming game where I was one of the Kings of the Homecoming court, along with my homies in my crew. We made up the entire Black Homecoming court. There was a White Homecoming court also, as if it was the year was 1952 and not 1992. It was what it was, I guess. That didn't matter to me at all because I was riding high. All the dreams that a twelve-year-old could have, came true. If only I could have this moment for a lifetime.

Chapter 6: Take Flight

1993 was my first year of high school. My freshman year was epic on so many levels. The school year would offer me a plethora of girls from three different cities. I was in a teenager's heaven. My crew consisted of the usual suspects. Somehow we managed not to bump heads or step on toes, at least among ourselves when we were on the hunt for girls. A plus for Drake and I was our cousin Sean, who was a graduating senior that year. Early on, he had co-signed us in the senior hallway, taking us under his wing. He would introduce us to all the hot senior girls in his class. Sean would tell all the guys in his senior class that we were off-limits to any of the freshman pranks they were notorious for unleashing. "You will have to deal with me if you prank these two. Don't get yourself fucked up." He said, bragging to his boys about us. That's when I saw her walk by. She had this long ebony hair that flowed with each stride she took, well taken care of caramel skin and the whitest smile, topped off with dimples. I would find out later her name was Sasha Evans. She was one of the smartest girls in the entire school. "Hey, pay attention." Sean said, snapping me out of my daze.

After our initiation, Drake and I searched for our homie Thurgood, who was a junior that year. He had the brand new

Volkswagen Jetta and was one of the star players on the football team. He showed us around and introduced us to a few of his friends.

The following days were laid back as we had the first week to adjust to our surroundings. My homie Kaiden and I took advantage of this time and recorded a demo tape to shop to the major labels. We had won a rap competition over the summer and were signed to this small independent label. One of their artists had a single on the radio.

During the lunch periods at school, we traded rhymes with whoever had a cypher going. Banging on the lunchroom tables or banging on the heater system in the hallway gave us the instrumental we all needed to draw a crowd and show off our freestyle skills. We had great respect for the culture of hip hop and each other. At one of our pop up rhyme sessions, I saw Sasha in the crowd, right as the bell had rung for the next period. "Hey, that was pretty good back there." She said with a look of being impressed on her face. "Thanks, I…" I said, before being cut off by a teacher who needed Sasha's help with something meaningful. In the couple of days of high school, I had secretly fallen for Ms. Sasha Evans, even though I knew she was out of my league.

It wouldn't take long for me to fall for another lady by the name of Mary Jane or by her government name "Marijuana." One day, Drake and I headed over to the Brewer Brothers to get the usual routine shape up. They had set up the barber equipment at a neighbor, and we had just made it inside before they decided to close shop for the day. "Yo, y'all the last two for the day." one of the brothers said. "Good, we made it just in time." I said, dapping up everyone in the room as we took our seats. Three guys, who would later become my friends and brothers, Arron, Cederio, and Jamal, were ahead of us and had used their time waiting for haircuts to roll up a total of ten blunts. Up until then, I had only smoked a little piece of a joint, which gave me a buzz, of course, but I wouldn't be what you would call a "smoker." All of that was about to change.

Cederio threw one of the freshly rolled blunts into my lap. "Yea, we about to smoke this motherfucker out!" he said while lighting up one himself. All of them? I thought to myself as I lit up mine. Before I knew it, all seven of us had a blunt, taking a tote until it was time to pass and receive the next one. This continued for a while as we talked about the usual things. The entire room was filled with smoke. Little clouds of cheba floated around and laid an overcast on the room. I was on cloud nine, trying not to fall asleep when I was called for next in the barber's chair. I could barely stand up. "Damn, look at your eyes boy." One of the Brewer Brothers said, handing me a mirror. Not only were they red, but they were also bloodshot burgundy red. Also, they were super glossy. "Your dad is going to beat your ass when you get home!" he said with a chuckle. "Nah, I got that covered." Arron said, loaning me his bottle of Visine. I used a couple of drops and returned it to Arron. "Ight, time for round two." Jamal said as he stood up from the barber's chair and lit the first of the remaining blunts.

He hit three times and passed it to me as I took my seat in the barber's chair. I took it reluctantly as I was already high. How high are we trying to get? I thought as I took my seat on the never-ending reefer train. Just then, Arron's older brother came inside looking for Arron. "Man, y'all got it smoked out in here." He said, grinning from ear to ear. "Where it at?" I was more than glad to pass it to him. I could barely keep myself from falling asleep. One look at me had him break out into a laugh. "Oh shit, you got the young boys fucked up around here. He inhaled on the blunt between laughs. "Your Pop," pointing at me, "and your Momma," pointing at Drake, "gonna beat y'all ass for being high." He said as his final retort. The Brewer Brothers chimed in. "We told em." They said, adding to the laughter. When I was done with my haircut, I took my seat back on the couch. It wasn't too long before I had blacked out. I could hear everything around me, although it was muffled; I couldn't make out who was who. My eyes were so heavy, as I struggled to open them, I found I could barely move my feet. Oh, I'm too high, I thought to myself. When I finally got my eyes to open, I could see Arron's brother giving his girlfriend a shotgun through the nose, but he looked like the devil. I blinked my eyes a couple of times to adjust what I was seeing. I was as high as a Georgia pine tree as the saying goes.

When Drake and I finally left, we floated down the street and found we had a monster case of the munchies. We stopped at a fast food place and ate until we had our fill and laughed at the most inappropriate things our teenage minds could imagine. We were "nice," a term we would add to our vernacular describing how high we were. After that day, it was official. I was now a stoner. Out of all the side effects that come with abusing marijuana the way we did, only one would be detrimental to me. I would develop a severe case of the "Fuck its." My wanting to make As and Bs in all my classes fell victim first.

"Fuck it." I could do the minimum and get Cs and Ds. Me wanting to continue playing saxophone and piano: "Fuck it." I'll quit that and focus on rapping. I was able to keep my stoner self away from my parents. Around the time progress reports came out, those Cs and Ds had turned to Es and Fs. The As and Bs helped bring my average to a D. This was alarming to my mother, who noticed some changes in my behavior and knew it would show in my academics. I had to raise my grades and do so fast. So, I signed up for tutoring after school. "Hey there, pretty eyes." A voice said from behind me as I turned to see who had made sure to get my attention. I realized it was... "Hey, Sasha, are you my tutor?" I said, showing all enthusiasm for the idea. "No, I just finished my session." She said matter of factly. I seized the moment and made small talk as I walked her to the door. Sasha gave no signs of knowing that I was a puppy for her love. "Well, see you around." She said, waving goodbye, flashing a smile. One day I saw Sasha at her locker. We started a little friendly conversation when I noticed her rubbing her neck.

"Let me get that for you." I said slyly, jumping at the chance to give her a massage. "Oh, thank you." She said appreciably, letting me continue, "Coach Jackson worked us like dogs yesterday at practice." "Practice?" I asked, concentrating more on her neck than her words. "Yes, track and field." She said while guiding my hands across her neck. "Hey, you should try out. We could use a lot of help for guys." "I think I will." I said half-heartedly. "Today?" Sasha asked excitedly. "Today, after school, I'll be there." I managed to say right as the bell rang. "Ok, see you there." She walked on to her next period class. Suddenly, I cared a great deal about track and field.

I threw on my P.E. clothes as quickly as I could after my tutor session and headed down to the track field. I was tempted to take a hit of the blunt before tryouts, but I decided not to when I saw Sasha stretching on the football field. She signaled me to come over to her. "You made it!" she said while doing her warm-ups. "Great, now help me stretch." She said with a laugh, grabbing my hands. While lying on her back, she lifted her left leg up to me to apply pressure to it. I looked down at her beautiful body. I began to daydream of us knocking the boots right there on the football field. My daydream was interrupted by a loud whistle being blown. "Alright, let's get started people!" the coach said through his megaphone. "Gotta go. Good luck on tryouts." She said as she jogged to the other side of the football field. I stared at her butt as it bounced around in her gym shorts until I felt a huge hand plant itself on my neck. "Well, if it ain't Hoop's son." The coach said while shaking me back and forth in his mighty grip. "How is he these days?" This is sweet. A little nepotism goes a long way, I thought as I continued the conversation with the coach. "Ok, good to hear man. I'm going to go extra hard on you then, son...I know what you're made of!" He blew the whistle again, deafening me for a moment. "Ok, up and down the bleachers, twenty times! Let's GO! Let's GO!" I took off for the bleachers.

As the day of tryouts came to an end, I was sore, tired, hungry, and was so ready for the day to be over so that I could finally spark the blunt I had in my bookbag. As I walked my way up to the sidewalk back to the building, Sasha pulled up and blew her horn. "You need a ride?" she asked, knowing the answer already. The soreness and feening were all worth it. "Sure." I said, giving her the biggest smile that capped the tremendous excitement behind it. I gave her directions to my house, and on the way, we talked about school and track. I was beside myself. I, a freshman, was getting a ride home from Sasha Evans, one of the hottest female seniors at my school. I played it cool as a milkshake on the drive to my house. When she pulled up into the driveway, I couldn't help but feel like I had a good chance of her feeling the same way I felt about her. "Well, see you tomorrow." I said as I got out of the car. "Yes, see you tomorrow." She said, flashing her million-dollar smile at me again. I waved her off as she drove out of the driveway. I reached down into my bookbag and retrieved the blunt. "I almost forgot about you." I confessed to the blunt, lighting it up and exhaling the white smoke through my nostrils with satisfaction.

The next few weeks went on like that. I was starting to like track and field as well. The coach wanted me to run the second leg in the relay race after qualifying for the long jump. Sasha and I would talk on the phone after she would make it home from dropping me after practice. We weren't a couple. The hierarchy of high school social status would make that impossible. However, we liked each other in that way. I hadn't smoked weed in three days. Sasha was keeping me high all on her own with her kisses and hugs. One day, I made the mistake of leaving my gym bag at home and spent most of the day trying to find a pair of running shoes I could borrow. "Coach is going to fry my ass." I explained to Sasha. She came up with the idea of just telling him before practice to save face. "Good idea." I said as I planted a kiss on her cheek before rushing off to tell him what had happened. Coach gave me the ok to not dress out for practice as he needed people to fish out the hurdles and pole vault equipment in the gymnasium. Later that day, I helped Sasha stretch before practicing her 4x4, letting her know I would be hauling equipment all day. "Aww, lucky you." She said, blowing a kiss at me before joining the others. I watched her jog away and then headed back to the building. The lobby of the school was empty and quiet. Maybe a few of the student body were scattered here and there, but for the most part, the building was vacant. I could hear footsteps behind me as I turned the corner toward the gym.

I sped up so that I could escape whoever had caught a glimpse of me, not sure if it were a teacher who would give me a hard time. I made it to the gym door handle when someone said, "What are you up to? Aren't you supposed to be on the track field?" I froze in my tracks, ready to give them my official statement of helping the coach with equipment alibi. It wasn't a teacher, but a student, a senior matter of factly. Her name was Conchita. She was of the loud and obnoxious variety. "Oh, you scared me." I said, giving out a sigh of relief. "Uh huh, you were probably in here fucking one of these hot in the ass females." She suggested as she walked up and got in my face. "Not today." I said, taken back by her stance and her grabbing my dick through my jeans. Before I knew what had happened, there we were in a bathroom stall of the boy's bathroom with our shorts and underwear around our ankles, having sex. As I rammed her from behind, she held on to the back of the toilet, trying not to make any noise to alert anyone of what we were doing; after ten minutes of pounding her over the toilet seat, I came to climax, and she had to cover my mouth to keep me from being so loud. We walked away from the bathroom in secret.

I felt a mix of enjoyment and guilt as I returned to the track and field with some of the equipment. I acted as if nothing had just happened. It wasn't supposed to happen like that, I thought. I just lost my virginity to Conchita of all people in the stall in a bathroom. "Gross!" I said out loud in disgust with myself. I thought about Sasha and how this was going to ruin everything with her. It was supposed to have been with her I kept thinking over and over as I watched her practice. I was overwhelmed by the desire to get high. I left the field that day without telling Coach or Sasha. It would be my last time on the track team that year. I felt like a complete loser. I needed to get high and forget everything else. A couple of weeks went by, and the phone calls between Sasha and me came to an end. She had started dating some guy on the track team once I had quit. I would see them all hugged up in the hallway at lunch. I was too jealous of him; he was dating the girl that was supposed to make me a man. The coach said I should try out again next year after telling him I couldn't continue running for him that year.

Now my afternoons were boring after school because all my friends were in sports. I spent plenty days just sitting on my front porch, smoking by myself. Sometimes, I would see Conchita walk by, and she would offer me more of her body. I took the liberty of finishing up my blunt before inviting her into my house.

As the school year progressed, so did my bad habits. All the weed I would smoke and the studio sessions to record our demo took their toll on my allowance. I hardly ever worked with my dad, now that I was in high school. I wasn't old enough to get a job, so I thought of creative ways to make money. There was this tree in my front yard whose leaves looked a little like weed. I had the idea to bag some of it up and sell it to the White boys at my school. They didn't know any better and would return the next day to buy even more. This was profitable, yet short-lived. Once the White kids realized that they just had a headache instead of a weed high, they found another dealer. One day out of boredom, I decided to ramble around in my parent's bedroom closet. They kept all types of things from the sixties in there. As I was going through some old records, I accidentally knocked a brown paper bag onto my head. I picked it up to put it back in its place, only to discover it was filled with crisp one hundred dollar bills, in stacks of thousands. "What the fuck!?" I said out loud as I stared into the bag of money. I thought long and hard about where the money came from and what it was for. My parents had several bank accounts, so to see this amount of cash stuffed into a paper bag and stashed onto a shelf in their bedroom closet was off-putting. I decided it had to be for something important and placed the bag where I had found it, but not before taking a single one hundred dollar bill from one of the stacks.

Chapter 7: Crack Experiment

After Conchita had taken my virginity, she and I would have sex regularly. We crept around mostly in the afternoon right after school. I wasn't interested in talking or going out with her. Our sex-capades were about busting a nut, and I made sure we had that understanding. To my surprise, Conchita was ok with our secret rendezvous. Apparently, it was just about sex with her too. I never told her that she had taken my virginity that day as she assumed I knew what I was doing in the sheets. My room would smell so bad after she and I did the damn thing. After she would leave, I would open the windows to my bedroom and spray as much air freshener as I could to cover the odor of hot funky sexy that made its way from my bedroom to the rest of the house. Vivian would beg me to start taking her somewhere else as the smell was that bad of a thing to witness. After washing my sheets or towels through the week, I decided to start meeting her over at her house.

On one of our secret hookups, I went over to Conchita's house as we had agreed at four o'clock. I found myself there a little earlier than we had planned but decided to see if she was ready for me anyway. I knocked on the door and Conchita's younger sister Courtney opened the door. "Hey, is Conchita here?" I asked, surprised to see her answer the door. "No, not yet." She replied, just as shocked to see me at the door. Courtney was the complete opposite of her sister. Whereas Conchita was loud and brash in demeanor, Courtney was more laid back and chill. We had shared a couple of laughs on the school bus in the past. "You can come in and wait for her though. She should be back in a little." She said, holding the door open, inviting me inside. I decided to wait. After waiting for ten minutes or so, I became impatient. I need some pussy, I said to myself. "Tell Conchita I..." I said, stopping mid-sentence. Courtney was bent over in front of me, appearing to do something to the television. I never noticed until now how great of a body she had. She wore these homemade jean shorts that barely concealed her thick thighs in the denim. Courtney stood there in front of me in this bow-legged stance. I was eye level to the three-inch gap between her legs. "Huh...tell her what?" she asked, still bent over, now looking me dead in the face. Seconds later, we were in her bedroom. I had all but ripped her clothes away as I dropped my pants down to my ankles. I lifted both of her legs, holding her by the ankles, and commenced to punish her with my wild thrusts and hard grinds. I left their house shortly after, giving Courtney what I had intended to give to her sister. With still no sign of

Conchita, I had got what I had come for after all. As I walked back to my house, I lit the spliff I had been saving for afterward. "Oooooweee!" I said with a laugh, taking a long tote on the reefer.

Basketball season had begun, and the games were known to bring people out. The first game of the season was the coming Friday. It was to be followed by a dance put on by the senior class to raise money. It had been a while since I got cleaned up and hung out with my homies. I would most definitely be in that building for both. My social status depended on it, I felt. I went to my parents' closet and took another one hundred dollar bill from the brown paper bag. That afternoon, Thurgood and I went to the mall to buy a new pair of sneakers. After I copped the overpriced kicks, got something to eat, and gave him gas money for the ride, I was flat broke again and had not completed putting together a fresh new ensemble for the game and the dance. The next day, I went back to the paper bag ATM in my parents' closet and removed two hundred of the crisp dollar bills from the stash. Ok, I swear this will be the last time, I thought to myself as I put the paper bag back into place on the top shelf. I was in the middle of calling a cab when the doorbell rang. It was a kid I was cool with from school who had just stopped by because he was in the neighborhood. It would be his lucky day. "Yo, you trying to ride to the mall with me?" I asked casually. He held a look of confusion on his face but managed to say. "Yea, but I don't have any—" "I gotcha; don't worry about it." I said, interrupting his upfront plea.

We smoked a good size joint as we waited for the cab to arrive. During the entire trip to the mall, I could see the cab driver looking into his rearview mirror, sizing me up. He and my companion both thought about how I was going to pay for the fare. I laughed to myself at the thought. "You young men don't plan on jumping out of the cab without paying, are you?" the cabbie finally asked as we approached the mall parking lot. We hopped out of the cab, and I handed him a bill and waited for my change. As we walked inside the mall, the kid asked me if I was selling dope. I shrugged off his question. "I need jeans and a shirt. Let's go in here real quick." As we made our rounds to the clothing store and then on to the video game store, coming out with this new fighting game that was supposed to be more realistic called Mortal Kombat, we found ourselves in the food court. I ordered food for us when he finally asked, "Hey, man, you think you could buy me a pair of shoes...I see you got it like that?" I counted the remaining money I had from my splurge. "No doubt. I told you I gotcha." I retorted, giving him a dap in reassurance. After we got him his pair of shoes, we were good to start our voyage home. We found a place to take some quick puffs of the half-smoked joint as we waited for the cab to drive up. When we got back to our town, I got off with the kid at his stop to avoid my dad seeing a taxi pull up in the driveway. The kid gave me my props for looking out for him the whole day. Our friendship had just received a booster shot in the arm. The next day at school, I saw him showcasing his new shoes to some other kids. He filled them in on the weed, and the cab ride over to the mall as well. Little rumors of me selling dope or weed started to buzz around the school. I did as much as I could to clear my name, but in the back of my mind, I knew it was good PR.

The game and the dance that Friday was amazing; still other Fridays just like that came and went. Withdrawals from the paper bag in my parents' bedroom closet came and went just as fast. I stayed popping tags on the newest Tommy Hilfiger or Ralph Lauren. I would have no less than two hundred dollars in my pocket at school, though only pulling out my knot of twenties and tens in the lunch line. Life was good. Kaiden and I had finished the demo, and the label was shopping it to whoever would listen. My grades improved with just enough effort on my part when the report cards came around again. I had a couple of girls giving me a great conversation, and my cousin Kaiden, who had been in juvenile, had just made it home from completing his sentence. I decided to pay him a visit in the projects one day after school. He told me to meet him in the woods, right outside of the entrance. "Caca Caca." I let out one of our birdcalls from back in the day. He replied in the same manner, giving me the whereabouts to his location.

My cousin hadn't been home for more than a week, and here he was in our old fort from when we were kids. As I walked into the old collapsed tobacco barn, I could feel the tenseness that was only outmatched by the overwhelming smell of chemicals. "What's up, cuz?" Kaiden greeted me with a dap and a half hug. "I can't call it." I replied. While taking in the scenery, I noticed from out of the corner of my eye this kid from a different neighborhood looking out of place. "What's up with him?" I asked my kinfolk. "Nothing, he's just scared as hell. I told him it wouldn't do anything." Kaiden said, aggravated with what was going on.

His answer confused me even more. I changed the subject. After a brief catching up, Kaiden went back to concocting in his makeshift laboratory. "What the hell are you making?" I finally asked. "Oh, just some dummy rocks to serve later tonight." He said as a matter of fact, then burst out laughing. I laughed along, having no clue what he was talking about. The kid in the corner who hadn't said a word since I had been there, started to look more nervous as my cousin laughed on. "Let me see?" I said, still laughing and clueless about what was going on. He placed four little cube-sized things into the palm of my hands. One was made of some kind of cheese covered in some tooth numbing gel. The other was a box of lye soap covered in paint. Then it dawned on me. By "dummies," he meant "fake," and by "rocks," he meant "crack." "I have more where that came from." He said proudly.

"Now that I have a tester, I can see which ones will work." The kid in the corner started to cry. "Shut the fuck up! You fucking pussy!" Kaiden yelled, walking over to the kid who was sobbing uncontrollably. I was in total awe, and I felt sorry for the kid. "So how much do you think you make from them?" I asked, trying to keep it cool so both of them would calm down. "Eighty to a hundred." My cousin said as he worked a car antenna into a crack stem. I looked over at the kid. "Please don't make me smoke that, I could die." He begged in between snot bubbles.

Kaiden walked over to where the kid sat on a bucket. "I swear to God if you don't stop crying, I'm going to beat your ass!" He said while pushing one of his artificial crack rocks into the opening of the stem. I couldn't watch this go down, and I couldn't stop it from happening. "Smoke this!" Kaiden said, as sternly as a parent would say, "take this" while forcing medicine down a child's throat. "You don't have to smoke it all, just enough to tell me if it numbs your mouth." He said to the kid, reassuring him. I couldn't believe what I was seeing. At first, I found this to be somewhat funny. Seeing my cousin bully someone way bigger in stature than him. Then, I was amazed at the level of criminal mindedness my cousin was operating on.

Now I was just afraid for this kid who had no choice but to play crackhead with my cousin. I looked away right before catching a glimpse of the kid's eyes pleading for me to intervene. "Smoke it God damn it!" Kaiden screamed violently. The kid took the stem, put it into his mouth, and lit the other end, holding the fake crack and inhaling the toxic fumes. The kid gagged from the smoke and was choking furiously, handing the stem back to Kaiden. "Did it numb your mouth?" Kaiden asked, more concerned about his experiment than the experimenter. The kid shook his head, indicating that it was a failure. "That was the cheese one. It should have worked." Kaiden said sparingly. He then began to fix another stem for the second trial. The kid started to look as if he would rather get beat up than to smoke another dummy. I could see him beginning to fidget around on the bucket. "Alright, smoke this one." Kaiden said, handing him the stem. "No!" the kid rebutted. He was finally standing up for himself, and I was glad to see him do it too. "No?" my cousin asked sarcastically, pulling out a .22 caliber pistol from his waist and placing it to the kid's head. Time seemed to stand still, then go in reverse, then forward to catch up with what had just happened. "Hey." I said softly, placing my hand on the opposite arm that held the gun, "I have a better idea than these dummies." Just then, the kid started to piss his pants. "Oh yea, what's that?" Kaiden said, still concentrating on the kid. "First, let's let this kid go...he won't tell anybody about this, right?" I said, directing my question at him. The kid shook his head no. "Alright then." My cousin said while putting the gun back on safety and into his waist. "Get the fuck out of here...and say no to drugs motherfucker!" he said, laughing while shoving the kid out of the abandoned barn. "Let's talk business." I said while lighting up a joint.

I left the projects that evening, relieved for that to be over. I had told Kaiden I would give him a hundred dollars tomorrow to buy real dope. He agreed to flip it and bring me back the hundred. I would be helping my cousin out and be able to start putting the money back. I thought, as I made my way back to my side of town. Saving that kid from my cousin was an afterthought. "Yo, shit is too crazy out here now." I said, laughing at what made that kid come with my crazy ass cousin in the woods in the first place.

My academics had taken a severe ass-whooping from all of my womanizing, weed-smoking rapper persona. All was not lost though. I continued to put some effort into making it to class and doing homework. The effort would leave me with a C average for the semester. It was enough to pass the ninth grade. I was just ready for the summer. Then I could focus on more important things, money.

Chapter 8: A Smile To Appreciate

The summer of 1994 was a hot one. Out of every car window, you could hear DJ Clue's Summertime Shootout blaring from the car stereo. By now, my cousin Kaiden had worked his way up to an ounce of crack. He was making a name for himself uptown. I was able to keep my name out of the mix of flipping crack. Months had gone by, and my parents hadn't said one word about money being missing from the paper bag. I wasn't able to put any money back, but I had stopped taking from it. My homie Kaiden and I had started receiving letters about our demo. We were holding on for a label to give us the call and not leave us with the usual "You guys are southern rappers rapping like New Yorkers" line. Out of frustration, Kaiden went to his dad's place back in Connecticut for the summer. We decided to pick up recording in the fall.

I was mowing the lawn one morning listening to the Wu-Tang Clan on my Walkman, thinking about what I was going to get myself into later that day. As I took a break to grab some water, I noticed my neighbor's granddaughter was being dropped off for what looked like the entire summer due to her excessive luggage. I noticed her noticing me, and we never seen each other before. She was gorgeous with this dark complexion that looked like milk chocolate. Small in the waist and thick in the behind. We waved and smiled at each other. This could get real interesting, I thought as I started mowing the lawn again, unpausing "Bring Da Ruckus" on my tape deck.

After days of flirting with one another from across the street, we finally met face to face. Her name was Mia. She had the prettiest smile, one her boyfriend didn't seem to appreciate. It turns out she was seeing a kid from my neighborhood. He and I were cool but not homies, so I kicked a couple of lines her way. Mia gave her relationship more respect than I had. She would say she was flattered by my advances but couldn't or wouldn't take me up. I pressed her every day about coming over. My cousin Kaiden called me one day and said that we should buy some guns and a car. He said he knew a guy we could get them cheap from. It sounded like something that we needed, so I had him set up a meeting, and I would have the money. The guns I understood, because we only had the raggedy-ass .22 pistol that would jam up. The car I wasn't so gung ho about. We were only fourteen. We met up that weekend to look at it. "We're only looking at the car." I reminded myself and my cousin. It didn't take long for me to be convinced that getting this car would allow us to do what we wanted and go where we wanted. "Five hundred cash." The owner of the car said. It wasn't much to look at. The car was a beat-up Honda Civic that had hundreds of miles already on it. It had a shoddy paint job, with a shoddy transmission to boot. It was, however, a five-speed.

"I'll take it." I said, handing him over the money. He counted the bills in disbelief. The guy could only have been about twenty years old himself, and the fact that he was selling a bunch of fourteen-year-olds a car had to have been stressful for him. "The title and all that is still in my name, so be careful with it." He said, stuffing the money into his pocket. He gave the keys to me and my cousin, and I climbed into our car. "I don't know what y'all little niggas up to." He said, taking a drag of his cigarette, "but y'all little niggas got it going on!" tapping the hood of the car as we drove off. Our first trip in the car was successful. We met the gunrunner in a neighboring city, buying from him a twelve gauge sawn-off shotgun, a nine-millimeter Glock, and a brand new .22 to replace the old one. We were living out our gangster and hustler fantasies and had no idea what we were getting ourselves into nor the amount of danger we were already in.

As the summer progressed, Mia and I started to see more of each other. She and Vivian had become friends over the passing weeks, and she was over our house all the time. I made sure I was at home if only to say hello before I headed uptown. I would practice my freestyle rhyme by setting up the video camera in my room, recording myself go bar for bar over my favorite instrumental at the time. "That was good!" Mia said, standing in my doorway. She caught me off guard, and I stumbled around, trying to stop the recording and my blushing. "Oh hey...how long were you standing there?" I asked, embarrassed by my lackluster performance. "Long enough..." she said, beaming at me. Mia had been complaining to Vivian how she hardly ever saw her boyfriend and when she did see him, he always had his homies with him. I used that bit of information to make my move finally.

I grabbed Mia by the waistline and pulled her closer to me so that our hips would collide. She stared at me with her beautiful brown eyes, unable to say anything. I started kissing her passionately on the lips, and I could feel her body going limp into my arms. My hands found a way to break our fall as we fell on top of my bed. Later that night, after I had gotten high and ate dinner, I rewound the tape of my freestyle. After watching several minutes of me rhyming into the camera, the tape continued to play until it caught up to where Mia and I had started kissing. It then showed where the camera had been knocked down as we crashed on my bed, recording every minute of our rendezvous. My jaw dropped as I turned the volume down on the remote. "Oh shit." I said with a grin. I got closer to the television to hear the audio without having it so loud. I watched in amazement at my own ass laying it down on tape.

The next day, Drake came over, and I just had to show him the footage. We smoked our usual afternoon blunt and watched the sex tape. It was the type of perverted humor only a teenage boy in the nineties could relate too. We laughed and gawked at the positions I had Mia in until the film ended with me breaking down the bed's headboard. "You wild boy." Drake finally managed to say between laughs. "Yo, I didn't know my stroke was that strong!" I said, still recovering from our laughing.

A couple of days later, some kids asked me about renting "the" tape. I wholeheartedly thought they were talking about the music until it occurred to me that they specifically asked to rent the tape and not buy it. "I'll give you two dollars."

One kid bargained. "I'll give you five!" another said, flashing the money in my face. "Wait, y'all know about the sex tape?" I said, losing all chances to deny any such tape existed. "I'll give you twenty dollars for it!" a familiar voice said from behind me. I turned to see it was the kid my cousin Kaiden had volunteered to play a crackhead that one day. "Come with me." I told him, taking the $20 out of his hand. It didn't take long for the news of this sex tape to spread around my town. It ended up being bootlegged, and that copy somehow ended up in the VCR of an adult. This adult demanded to know who the stars of this now pornographic production were.

Needless to say, our parents were notified, and they decided to have a meeting with Mia and I, front and center. There was this calm before the storm as we all gathered in my living room after a drizzle of rain followed by dark skies and lightning. The climate in my living room was ideal for twister weather. I felt so sorry for Mia because her parents now knew she wasn't a virgin. I'm sure the circulation of our accidental lovemaking didn't do the same for her popularity as it had done for mine. If I were high, it would have been blown by the end of this meeting of families. "Do you love my daughter?" Mia's father asked. I looked at Mia, who was overly done with my presence by now but managed to look at me as her father waited for my reply. "I like her a lot...she is smart and funny...I don't love her." I said as my voice tapered off at the end of my statement. After Mia and her parents left my house, I didn't see her for the rest of the summer. My parents laid into me on their own for the next couple of days. Here I was again, grounded for yet another summer.

The ordeal had become the talk of the town. A year later, people were still talking about it. The now infamous sex tape spread like wildfire. I was amused as women twice my age would give me a certain look when they saw me in the street. My mind was elsewhere; to be exact, it was on my money. The first day of school came and went with the usual commencement. It was the fall of ninety-five. My cousin Kaiden started to lose his focus.

My aunt Marcie had discovered all the new shoes and clothes he had in his room. When she questioned him about it, he told her the clothes were mine and that he had borrowed them. This made no sense as I was twice his size, but it provided a temporary cover for the moment. Kaiden had also started to flash his money around uptown, showing off his wads of cash to people that wouldn't hesitate to rob him as they eventually did. Kaiden had been in a shootout where fortunately, no one was injured or killed. However, he was robbed at gunpoint by some out of towners. He assured me he wouldn't allow it to happen again and that they only took a thousand off of him. I had started to regret getting him involved in flipping the money. He was getting more and more reckless. I'll deal with my cousin later, I thought.

That night my homie Kaiden and our rap entourage would be taking his mom's car to this new nightclub that had opened up in a nearby city. It was an eighteen and up Hip-Hop club that everybody was talking about. Every teenage male or female that had a reputation was there last weekend. I was told it was a who's who type of party, so we had to be there this weekend. Slipping the doorman an extra twenty was all the proof of being eighteen that you needed to get in. The club that night was packed to capacity. The DJ was killing his set with "Bam Bam" by Sister Nancy. My entourage made our way over to the bar, looking for someone old enough to buy beer for us. I bumped into my cousin Kaiden doing the same thing. We placed our orders and made our way back over to the speakers. "Kaiden, you know Kaiden." I said, making an unnecessary reintroduction to my cousin and homie. We laughed as my cousin waved over his band of gangsters. "Yo, y'all drove the car here?" I asked, counting heads. "Yea! Good thing we bought the straps too. I just saw that nigga who robbed me." I could have jumped out of my skin as I listened to my cousin's words over the music. I knew that he had thoughts of getting him back in mind. The stack was long gone, but revenge would be his for the taking. "Don't do this here, man." "Wait until after the club is out, and then handle your business." I said sharply.

The beers had come just in time. "Ok." Kaiden said while taking a bottle out of the case. He knew I was right in basically telling him not to ruin the festivities. The party continued to escalate; girls were everywhere. They seemed to be falling from the roof. My cousin Kaiden and crew had found a spot of their own to post up in. Now and then, I'd scan the crowd to see how he was coping. "Y'all be waiting for me to drop this one all night!" The DJ said, finishing up a couple Go-Go records and proceeding to drop the needle on Junior M.A.F.I.A.'s "Get Money." The entire club went ballistic. I hit the dance floor with a beer in hand, reciting the lyrics to find me a dance partner. I grabbed up this cutie, and we two-stepped with each other reciting the chorus in unison.

"Fuck niggas...get money. Fuck bitches get money." After a couple of songs, my dance partner and I sat down and started with the introductions.

Just then, a fight broke out, and security broke through the crowd. I stood up, trying to see who it was but couldn't over all the people in the crowd. Moments later, security walked back through carrying a dude that appeared to be dazed outside, and the party came back to a roar. I asked someone walking by what happened. "Your cousin Kaiden wilding out. He threw a beer bottle and split this guy's forehead wide the fuck open!" he said with amusement. "Looks like he has a pussy on his forehead." A walker by chimed in. I stood there shaking my head in disbelief. Maybe this was a good thing, I concluded. I tried to find my cousin to see what condition he was in, but he was nowhere to be found. I made my way back over to where my crew was just in time to hit a blunt that was in circulation.

Moments later, the guy with the bleeding vagina of a wound on his forehead walked back through the door he was carried out of. I couldn't take my eyes off of him as I followed him around the club, asking people who had hit him with the bottle. One guy he stopped to asked appeared to have said,

"Some nigga named Kaiden." The guy then started to ask, "Where was Kaiden?" All the while looking super vexed. As I watched this play out, some relief came to me. Kaiden wasn't even in the club, I thought. I laughed to myself until that guy was coming straight for where we were standing with his eyes on my homie Kaiden.

Just as he was about to smash his fist into the unexpecting face of my rap partner, I reacted with my haymaker of a punch, landing a blow to his already wounded head. The force behind my punch caused me to fall directly on top of the guy. Several fights broke out around and over us. I managed to come from under the sea of swinging fist and feet untouched as two security guards had snatched me up after I had started the fight. The police arrived inside and shut the party down. It was almost time for the club to shut down anyway, so the fight was just the finale for now tired and hungry club-goers. My cousin, however, had one last closing act. As the parking lot began to fill up as the club emptied, my cousin Kaiden and his crew took out their guns and started shooting up in the air. This caused everyone to scatter and run to their cars, ending the night like any other club night. That would be the first example of a good thing coming to an end.

Chapter 9: Black Sheep

"I told them I got the money from you and that you had found it!" My cousin Kaiden said frantically over the phone. I stood there, kicking myself. It was over. Kaiden had gotten sloppy after that night at the club, finding himself in more and more trouble. He had shot a crackhead, and the police were looking for him. My Aunt Marcie had gone into his room and found hundreds of dollars hidden with more clothes and shoes. Another one of our aunts had spotted him driving our car. When he got home, he was given the third degree by our uncle and his mom. "Fuck..." I was speechless. "They kept asking me if I were selling drugs, and I'm already fucked up." He said admittingly. My mind was racing already when I saw my uncle's car pull up in the driveway. "They're here, I gotta go!" I said, hanging up the phone. "Ok, think." I said, pacing back and forth. There was no way I could deny the story of finding the money. That was the truth and hell of a lot better than confessing to what we did with the money. We had made enough flips to put back the money I took from it. I hadn't, however, had the chance to put it back in the paper bag. I quickly took out three thousand from my stash spot in the box spring under my bed and put it inside an acoustic guitar. I could hear the doorbell ring as I closed the door to my bedroom. Exhaling and accepting my fate, I waited for the shit to hit the fan.

My uncle, an aunt, and my father took turns laying into me about how stupid and dangerous it was for me to tamper with the money I found. I gave them the best excuse I could muster in hopes of avoiding the other shoe dropping. They were relieved to hear that it wasn't that we were selling drugs. I told them that I had only taken out four thousand, bought the car and Kaiden and me some clothes and shoes, and the rest was in my room. "Is this all of it!" my dad asked sternly as I handed him the money. "Yes!" I said, not making eye contact with him. My mother, who had been quiet the whole time, was crying.

"You could have been killed!" she said through her sobbing. She was the only one of the adults who hadn't found any relief in my testimony. Maybe I wanted to die, I thought, as her voice played over and over in my head. All the talk about what could have happened to us rolled off my back like water off a duck. Things did happen, and we handled them accordingly. The thought gave me a sense of pride. The worst of my latest episode was over with the matter of confiscating the car and what to do with it. For days after that, my mother walked around in mourning of her middle child's innocence. Sure I got into trouble as a little kid, but this was startling for her. I felt horrible breaking her heart in that way. She hardly said a word to me, and when she did, the amount of pain I had introduced her to would show on her face. Kaiden ended up in prison after standing trial for shooting the crackhead. He caused a considerable amount of commotion after he received his sentence. Not one to cooperate, Kaiden ran out of the courtroom and across the street and somehow managed to climb to the top of a building. Hours later, the police talked him down and took him into custody. It would at least be twelve years later when I found out the real truth about the thirty thousand and some odd hundred dollars that I had stumbled upon.

After all that happened, I received the punishment that would carry me into the next school year. I had nothing but time on my hands. I thought back to all the horrible things I had done up until now. All the shame I had brought to my mother and father gave me this feeling that I couldn't shake. I felt that this was who I was, the black sheep of the family, the problem child, the hardheaded mischievous one. I brought my thoughts to my dad, who always seemed to know what to say. He listened as I told him my thoughts and how I felt about myself. "No one's perfect son." He said, placing his hand on my shoulder. "The only perfect person to walk this earth was Jesus Christ." That would resolve anything I talked about with him. "You're not a bad kid. I believe spending some time reading your Bible would help you make better choices."

Hearing him say I wasn't a bad kid cheered me up some, although I wasn't exactly sold on the whole "church boy" idea. I had worked hard to become this cool ass sophomore rapping guy. I couldn't just throw all of that away. "Don't worry about your mother." My dad said, interrupting my daydream. "She will come around to her old self soon. You may want to help out more around the house." He said with a guarantee. "Either way, she loves you. Plus, I love you and God loves you." He said before leaving me alone with his advice.

After much resistance, I did what my dad suggested and started to reread the Bible. I had to have been nine or ten years old the last time I opened the enormous red children's Bible. Even as a kid, the stories were just hard to believe. I was determined to give Jesus, Joseph, and Mary a chance. A new school year was starting, in which I was now a junior.

Our usual first day of school ritual hadn't lost its zeal. I had the idea of documenting our adventures of the first day of school smoke session and recording our rap cyphers between classes. When we arrived at school drunk and high, I cruised the hallway with the video camera filming everyone in their back to school freshness. I collected random faces, butts, and breasts of all the girls in my view. Someone had the idea of going down to see what the freshman girls looked like this year. We took the trek over to the freshman hall.

Nothing could have prepared me to come face to face with my actual first love. When we turned the corner acting like fools, all I could see was a sea of P.Y.T.s scattered about the place. Some of the girls made sure to get our attention so they would be on camera. That's what stood out most to me. She was different from her classmates, standing out by not standing out. "Here, I'll get this back from you after the third period is over." I said, passing the video camera off to a homie. I was taken away by her yellower than New York cheesecake skin tone. I noticed her struggling with the combination of her locker and decided to approach her, checking my breath as I thought of something clever to say. "Hi, it looks like you could use some help." I said with a grin. "Yes, I sure could." She said, frustrated. "What's the combination?" At that moment, our eyes met. I was taking in first by how beautiful she was. I would find out later that she was half Jamaican and half Irish. Her hair was cut in the all so popular Halle Berry hairdo, and she smelled so good. She was just as lost in my features as I was in hers, to the point of me having to repeat myself. "The numbers?" I asked again, obviously smitten. Once I got her locker open, she thanked me repeatedly as she didn't want to be late for class. I had the idea of continuing our conversation while I showed her to her homeroom, but her friends had shown up to do the same thing, so I improvised. "Here, take my number and call me after school, just in case you need help with anything else." I said while writing my phone number on the back of one of her notebooks. She said she would and told me her name was Kia. Her name was only a minor detail I had overlooked while I had thoughts of making her my girlfriend.

I was pretty much done with playing any sport when I entered my junior year of high school. All my homies were involved in some game that took up all their time, so I spent most of my days solo after school. A couple of weeks into the school year, Thurgood had introduced me to his homeboy Abdul, who had transferred to our school from New York. We hit it off immediately as we found we had the same taste in music, comic books, and of course, getting high. Kia and I had become a couple. My life slowed down considerably compared to the last school year of hustling. I found myself studying the Bible now instead of reading it.

The fact that my new boo was a devout Christian proved to help me cool my jets and try to atone for my past trespasses. I was back into my schoolbooks as well. I had stopped drinking, and if I did smoke, it would be before and after a Friday basketball or football game. Even sex had taken a backseat to my desire to walk the straight and narrow. When Kia and I were alone, it was a knee jerk reaction to jump her bones. Her commitment to God was greater than her promise to me as she was able to withstand her urges as well as my sexual advances. "Even though I do love you, I love God too, and he wouldn't want us to have sex before we were married." She would say when things got hot and heated. Guys would sometimes ask me if I was "hitting that," knowing with my reputation that I had to be. Girls would ask Kia the same thing for the same reason. We would proudly say that we weren't having sex but were practicing abstinence. It was the truth, so people that knew Kia totally believed us. The people that knew me couldn't believe it. I couldn't believe it myself. "I've been thinking of getting saved." I confided in Abdul one day. "Oh yeah?" he replied. "Kia still not going to give the panties son." He said, half-laughing. "I'm serious. I've been thinking about it a lot lately. It feels like the right thing to do." I said, trying to convince myself more than him. "With her, it's not even about sex." Abdul looked like he wanted to apologize, but he didn't. "I feel you...just make sure it's for all the right reasons." He said, signaling his approval. I volleyed with the idea of being saved and not being saved that night while I lay in bed. Why did getting saved and going to church to become what I would call a "church boy" seemed so ridiculous to me? How could any of that compare to getting money and having sex all while high or drunk, if not both?

All the kids I knew that went to church seemed to be envious of those of us that didn't go to church. They eagerly listened to our stories of "sinful fun" whenever they got the chance. What exactly were they saved from? I thought as I closed my eyes and fell asleep. The next day at school, I asked Kia about why she had chosen to get saved. She gave me this look, recognizing I was on the verge of taking the leap of faith. Choosing her next words wisely she said, "Well, my mother at first, kind of made me because she knew best. You see..." I looked up at her, and my facial expression exposed what I was thinking. Kia quickly countered. "But," she said, taking my hands into hers, "I'm glad she did, I may have never witnessed God's grace, mercy, and forgiveness if she hadn't." "Forgiveness?" I asked. "Yes, we are all sinners, including little ole innocent, naive me." She said, laughing. I couldn't imagine Kia any other way than she was now. "You're gonna have to tell me about sinning Kia one day." I chuckled. She promised me that she would help out in my transition and that our relationship would be blessed because of it, yet another approval in my decision to try on Jesus.

I decided I would give my life to Jesus before church that Sunday. The pastor's sermon was on salvation, with undertones of living free of sin, kept my attention throughout the program. He seemed to be talking to me directly. "Who among you in the congregation will answer the door? Jesus is knocking. Let him in." The pastor said as the choir and the pianist began another performance. I stood up and walked up to the altar, lowering myself to kneel on the first step and bowed my head.

Chapter 10: Relapse

My mother was so pleased with my decision to devote my life to God. She didn't say as much, but it showed on her face that day forward. Kia screamed in my ear over the phone when I told her the news. "Praise the Lord, my boyfriend is saved." She said, excited by the news of my submission. My whole family was happy and proud, as well. On the other hand, I was confused, being that I felt the same as I did before I had gone down in the baptizing pool. Not to alarm anyone or have them retract their showers of gratefulness, I decided to go with the flow. It would kick in, I thought, after a week or so has passed.

An entire month had come and gone. Things were at a minimum, ok. I had dipped into my stash of money and bought a couple of dress shirts and shoes. My excitement about this new Christian life started to wane once the routine of Bible study on Wednesday and service on Sundays began to settle in, especially once I had worn my church boy outfits a couple of times.

It became difficult to concentrate when I studied the Bible now. I found it odd because that didn't happen previously. Kia and I were going strong, but it seemed as if all we ever talked about was God or Jesus. If we did talk about us, it was in the context of us being married in the future. I started to miss those days of backsliding. The allure of getting high and drunk and having sex and running the streets began to take its toll on me. Over spring break, Kia had flown to Ireland to visit some relatives of hers. Her absence made it easier to slip back into some old habits. It started with first taking one or two totes of one of my buddy's blunts.

"I'll hit it only a couple times." I would say, denouncing the stoner persona I had been known for. That would morph into me taking a blunt to the head. A couple of harmless phone calls from some girls other than my girlfriend would lead to having one of them over for knocking the boots. I had found my way back to the crooked and wide path I had become so familiar with, all in a week's time. I had given up on saving my soul from total damnation. It didn't work for me, I thought. How could any of it be real? As I looked at myself in the mirror that I would look into as a little kid. Shaking my head at being so naive to think I could be anything other than what I was. While examining myself in the mirror, I decided that day that I was the black sheep of my family. Who are you? I asked myself repeatedly, gawking in the mirror for an answer. "I'm a hustler!" I finally said out loud.

"A gangster... a motherfucking player!" I continued hyping myself up. As I turned away from the mirror and flipped the light switch off, a thought resurfaced from the folds of my mind.

If I was indeed all of these things: a hustler, a gangster, a player, I knew I would be dead by the age of eighteen. "I can't wait to see you at school tomorrow, baby!" Kia said over the phone bubbling with excitement. I hadn't told her about the things I had done over the spring break. "Uh huh, me too." I replied flatly. "Are you ok? You seem different?" she asked with a trace of hurt in her tone. "I'm ok...hey, let me call you back." I said, hanging up on her without her response. It wasn't my fault I lost interest. If she had given me the sex, we would have been fine. I settled on the thought. I wouldn't have cheated. Stepping outside on my front porch, I noticed my neighbor Cederio in his front yard, talking to a crackhead. As I approached, he was ending his transaction. "Yo, just beep me tomorrow after three." My neighbor yelled as the feind walked off. "What's goodie?" I asked while slapping my hand into his. "Nothing much, man...about to light this L, you trying to smoke?" Cederio asked, already knowing the answer to his question. "No doubt, just what I needed." I said with relief.

We sat behind his house, out of sight, and smoked the blunt to completion. I asked him about the money he made from selling crack, acting as if I had no idea how it all worked. Cederio told me the prices and how he flipped his money to make more money. He became animated as he told me the ends and the outs. It hadn't dawned on him as to why I was asking him these questions. "You trying to get down with the team or something?" he asked while rolling up another blunt. "I don't know, maybe." I replied half-heartedly. "I gotta re-up tomorrow after school. Ride with me, and we will work out the details." He said while exhaling the marijuana smoke through his nostrils. "Ight, bet." I said, welcoming the second blunt as Cederio passed it to me.

The next day at school, I tried my best to avoid Kia, but she found me high and intoxicated in the hallway where I used to hang out. "Hey, I've been looking all over for you!" she said, obviously bothered by my failure to find her. "Oh, I figured I would run into you during the lunch period." I retorted. By the look on her face, Kia was no longer concerned about my whereabouts; her concern had shifted to my state of mind. "Are you Nice?" she demanded to know. I turned and looked at her before I spoke. I knew I had to do this now and there was no turning back. "Yeah...I'm as high as giraffe pussy right now." I said with a laugh, causing my homies to snicker and laugh. Our good time would be interrupted by her reasoning. "Why, after all you..." I couldn't allow her to finish. "I think we should break up." I said, returning her interruption.

The hallway stopped to a crawl as my words pushed out the sound of any other conversations nearby. "You're breaking up with me? But why?" she said, holding back tears. I couldn't answer her. I felt as if I had just stabbed her in the heart with a knife. I looked into her eyes and saw the pain I had given her. This is for her own good. I won't drag her down to hell with me, I thought. "I need some pussy...and you're not trying to give it...so!" I said, twisting the proverbial knife further into her. My final words were sobering for her. "Ok, if that's what you want." She said calmly as she walked away. I continued the show for those still watching. "Yes!" I shouted, "Free at last...now who trying to give up them draws!?" This earned me some laughs and a couple of new phone numbers from some random girls. Unbeknownst to me, it would also earn me years of regret and shame via karma.

As the day came to an end, word of our breakup had found its way to the gossip mill. I got all types of evil stares in my direction as I walked down the hallway to my locker. I had broken a good girl's heart, and nobody, except for my homies, was trying to be seen with me. I was alone in the junior hallway when she cornered me between my locker and the wall. "So, I heard that you were single now?" she said as she maneuvered her personal body space into my personal body space. Her name was Serafina, who was the total opposite of Kia. Whereas Kia was innocent and reserved, Serafina was forward and assertive. She had no problem walking up to me after hearing about my breakup and letting me know she wanted to give me what I was looking for. Everything about Serafina solicited sex to my underwhelmed spirit as we stood in the hallway. She was gorgeous. Her high yellow complexion complemented her bright red lipstick she covered her voluptuous lips with. Long and intricate braids covered half of her face, which only added to her mystique. She had mastered the makeup brush as she looked more like a college student than a sophomore in high school. She wore this too short of a blue dress and a halter top, so conforming to her breasts, they looked as if they would burst at the seams. I could only view this girl in sections at a time, as she was flawless. "You are single now, right?" She asked, breaking my concentration on her cherry red lips. "Yea, I umm me and my uh." I stammered. "Aww, I heard about it." She said as she took my hand and placed it up under her already revealing skirt. "I also heard you could use some of this?" she said, rubbing my hand over her crotch. All I could do was smile at her as she seduced me with her eyes and suggestiveness. "Here, take my number." She said as she scribbled her seven digits into my hand with a mascara pencil, kissing me on the cheek before walking away. I stood there stuck with a dumbfounded look as well as red lipstick on my face. Just then, Cederio walked up as I was still caught off guard by the devil in the blue dress. "You ready to ride, cuzo?" he asked.

Cederio was a lot of things to me. He was my next-door neighbor, my second cousin, and my homeboy. He would eventually be the person that showed me how to increase my hustle skill set in our little hometown. Cederio was a senior and had a promising future in either basketball or football, but like most of my crew, our thoughts on the future were limited to what would the new Nike Air max look like or whose daughter could we stick our dick in this weekend. That and how to make as much money as we could in as little time as possible. Cederio drove a classic Carolina blue 1969 Chevy Malibu that belonged to his grandfather. That car was notorious in our town and surrounding cities. If you saw this car, you knew that Cederio, Jamal, and Arron were in it, either already high or on their way to get high. "I gotta go to the crib first." Cederio said as we got inside the car. "Roll up." He said, tossing me a jar of hydro and cigar. I proceeded with splitting, dumping, and re-rolling the cigar as we sat in the afternoon school traffic. Cederio popped in a DJ Clue mixtape and turned the volume all the way up on the stereo. Once we were on the main highway, I ignited the reefer as we bobbed our heads to "How High" by Method Man and Redman. After a quick pit stop to pick up some money from our stash spots, we were back in the Malibu on our way to see his connect.

As we rode along the highway smoking and letting the bass from his speakers put us in a relaxed mode, my mind was filled with reefer smoke and dreams of building my money stash back up before summer. "I'm going to get a half an ounce. What you trying to get?" he asked, turning the volume down as we pulled up into his connect's driveway. I pulled out my wad of cash and counted. "Yea, I'll cop one too." I said, folding the rest of the money, putting it back into my pocket. He nodded in agreement, then reached up under the driver seat and retrieved a chrome .32 revolver. I pulled from under my shirt a .32 automatic, cocking it and putting it back in my waistline. "Just in case." He cautioned me. "I've never had to pullout, but...you never know." As we got out of the car and headed up to the front step, I took in my surroundings. The dope connect had an immaculate house. I imagined every house in the neighborhood looked like that, but I was sure that this was the only home purchased with blood money. The door opened, and Cederio and I found ourselves standing in the living room. The smell of food seeped from the kitchen, causing my already ravished stomach to tighten. The woman stirring the pot must have been the one who had let us in. She and Cederio carried on a dialogue that I could hear but wasn't paying attention to. Two little boys, no older than the age of eight, sat on a couch playing Sega Genesis. This is where we came to buy dope from? I thought to myself. Suddenly, a door was opened from the back of the house, exposing music blaring and a cloud of ganja. "Yo, back here!" a voice yelled out. Cederio hollered for me to follow him to the back of the house.

Standing in the hallway was a guy I had seen around town and in the nightclubs. He was older than us but not by too many years. "What's up Cederio?" He shouted over the music, extending his hand. "What's up? I'm chilling man. Came to get some work." Cederio replied. "Oh ok." The guy replied, looking directly at me. Cederio must have noticed his connect's concern about me being there. "This is my cousin." He offered the guy in exchange for his trust. I extended my hand, and his face lit up. "Oh, yea, the one that found all that money a while back?" He said, grabbing my hand to shake it. "Yea." I said with a laugh in my tone. Now properly introduced, we could get down to business. "Have a seat. Have a seat." The guy said as he retrieved a half-lit blunt from his ashtray. "So?" He said, puffing on the cigar, "What do you need from me? Two onions?" Cederio said while taking the blunt from the guy's hand. The guy reached over to a nightstand and retrieved a digital scale and a large china plate with huge chunks of crack cocaine. He carefully measured the pieces of crack, using a razor blade to cut smaller pieces if needed until he had bagged up our orders. We talked about the Chicago Bulls game as we paid the man and finished up our business. The guy made sure he gave me his pager number to beep him when it was time to re-up. "Y'all niggas got a tight little squad, man, be safe out here." He said, as Cederio and I got into his car and backed out of his driveway.

We took off toward the Italian pizzeria to finally give in to the munchies that provoked us since the first blunt we smoked. As we sat at the table, I couldn't help but feel like a character in one of those mafia movies. As the language and smells of a Sicilian life came from the kitchen, Cederio and I sat there at the table with guns on our person and packages of dope in the glove compartment of his car. I felt alive and empowered. This was the feeling I had been missing during my stint as a church boy. I could do this forever, I thought. When our strombolis were brought out to us, the jukebox began to play this song by Franco Battiato that urged me to get into character.

"Pauley..." I said to Cederio, wiping my mouth with my napkin, doing my best Robert De Niro impersonation. "I gotta thank you for introducing me to the Don. How can I repay you?" Cederio sipped his drink and smiled. "Fugetaboutit!" He said, being down for the charade. "Now Paulie, I owe you. I owe you big!" We laughed at how accurate the improv was to our real lives. "Yo, I really do appreciate you turning me on to your connect. Let's hit the mall up when we leave here to see what we can see." Cederio looked at me as to question my buying power. "And yea, I gotcha my nigga." I said, confirming I was going to splurge on the both of us. He nodded while holding back a smile. We finished our food and headed over to the mall, going from shoe store to shoe store until we ended up at a jewelry store. I counted out enough money to purchase us both 18K gold herringbone necklaces. We wore them right out of the store, making sure all the girls we passed got a good look at them. "You ight, Pauly." I told Cederio when we made it back home from our business and pleasure trip. "You ight too, Vinney." He answered back, holding up his gold chain. "A real stand-up guy!"

Chapter 11: The Darkside

It was official. I had become the best version of my darker persona. There was no resistance put up by my conscience to maintain any level of decency at this point. Everyone in my crew seemed to be on that same train of thought. We bumped heads often with guys in our school from the other cities. There would be these big brawls in the hallway with four or five guys exchanging blows while the teenage crowd cheered them on. The teachers and principle were helpless in preventing these brawls from happening. Eventually, the fights started the police presence policy to come into effect.

That wasn't enough to deter the fighting, but now not only would you be suspended for three days, you would also be arrested for fighting on the school property. Every other day, there was a word of so and so going at it, then being hauled off to jail. It got so bad that a riot started after these two White students got into a fight and were not punished in the same manner as other people. The students' mother was a teacher at our school, so people thought some nepotism was being played. The students were also two White females, so other people thought White privilege was being used as usual. Either way, the injustice of it all caused our school to riot and protest, promising not to return to class until justice was served. My friends and I used our time to get high, roam the halls, and bait girls to come with us to the theatre room.

I rarely studied anymore or made it to all of my classes but maintained a C average as exam time rolled around. English was still a breeze. I enjoyed that class, so I showed up for it. I held an A average in that subject. History was another subject that kept my attention. I was a wiz at remembering dates and names. I found it offensive to read about US history in our textbooks. The history teacher and I would debate about the lack of diversity in the textbooks, and that took up much of the class time, which my classmates loved. "Just remember this information, from this book for the test, would ya!?" he would say, basically waving his white flag in defeat. My C plus average and my debating skills kept me in good standing with the F.B.L.A. (Future Business Leaders of America), which Serafina had become a member of. We had become a couple and used the F.B.L.A. as a travel agency. Being that we lived in different towns, we only got to see each other at school or school events, such as during the F.B.L.A. field trips and conferences, which often meant we would be staying overnight. Serafina and I would find a way to have sex. Even at school, we would find some discreet way to bump uglies, even if people were around.

One day, as we sat with her friends outside on a picnic table during lunch, Serafina whispered in my ear, "I don't have any panties on." Sounding very much turned on by the fact. I looked at her and smiled like I had found a hundred dollar bill on the ground. "Really?" I asked. She nodded, confirming what she told me and what I had been thinking. "I'm going to sit in your lap, take your dick out, I'm going to fuck you right here." she said, licking my ear and returning to her conversation with her friends.

I unzipped my zipper and took out my manhood, as she requested. Leave it to Serafina to push the envelope and up the ante on our last sexcapade. She positioned herself on my lap and guided my penis in penetrating her as she sat down on my lap. I could feel her grinding on me as I looked away, pretending to be bored with all the girl talk. Serafina rocked back and forth on top of me. Our incognito lovemaking was interrupted by the lunch period bell. She stopped her gyration long enough for me to adjust myself and keep our cover. Serafina turned to face me and gave me an extra-long kiss, apologizing for not being able to finish what she started. "Oh lord. There they go again!" One of her friends said in a teasing way. "What? It's not like we were fucking." She said with her usual smirk.

It had become a routine now to hit the block right after school. Drake and I would smoke a blunt and then head our separate ways. I had acquired a beeper so that I could be reached when I wasn't on the block. I didn't like hugging the block, meaning just standing there looking like I was selling dope. My time in between hand to hand transactions would be spent writing rhymes and talking to Serafina on the payphone after she would beep me 911. Most of the time, by the time I got home from school, the feinds had already been "plucked" for their money. It would be in the wee hours of the morning when they would return with more money. I concluded that if I was going to make any money selling crack, I would have to sneak out of the house at night after my dad fell asleep by removing the screen from my bedroom window and pulling the blinds down over the window so that the screen appeared to be in place. This window of opportunity was only good for an hour or so. My mother would be returning home from work around midnight. I risked it all every time I climbed out of the window and headed uptown. My black army pants pockets concealed a blunt I had pre-rolled, a gram of crack cut into five twenties, a twenty-dollar bill, and a .32 pistol. My favorite was my C.D. player loaded with the latest mixtape. It would get me through the night and calm me down on my trek back home.

Once uptown, I sold my first twenty of dope. It wasn't long before I would be sold out. After giving my beeper number to the crackheads with instructions to page me after three o'clock for the scutter, I would be a hundred dollars richer, and it would only be thirty minutes that would have passed.

I would light up my blunt in delight as I walked back toward my house. I would take in the scene of the run-down shotgun houses and trash that surrounded me. As a kid, I used to be intimidated, yet intrigued by this part of town and the people that lived here. Who would have thought I would one day be standing in the middle of it, using it for my bidding. I would throw the hood from my hoodie over my head as I walked and smoked to the sounds of Black Moon's "Who Got Da Props." As my high would settle in, I could feel the vibration from my beeper. I would ignore it and keep my pace back to the house.

From time to time, I would see Kia in the hallways at school. Even though our breakup was pretty bad, we were able to salvage our friendship. She had moved on by now and was dating a good ole church boy. I was happy for her and him. Sometimes I would walk Kia to her French class that was taught by the school's basketball coach. The basketball coach didn't like me that much and would advise Kia to stay away from the likes of me. "He has it out for me, Kia." I tried explaining to her. "Why do you say that?" She asked surprisingly. "You do have a 'reputation' now and that girlfriend of yours..." She said, shaking her head. "You have changed a lot since the beginning of the school year. Please be careful." "I got this. I know what I'm doing Kia." I retorted. She smiled and disappeared into her classroom. I made my way back outside for the rest of my lunch period. A rap cypher was ending, but I had made it just in time to hit the tail end of a blunt that was lit right outside of the stairwell. Just as I was about to take a tote of the reefer, I could see the basketball coach's size fourteen loafers on the other side of the glass. My first reaction was to drop the roach clip and run before the basketball coach realized it was me standing there. We all scattered in several directions trying to avoid our faces being seen by the coach/teacher turned narc. I managed to make it to my next period class and was relieved I still had a little buzz left. About thirty minutes into class, the principal came over the intercom asking for me to report to his office. When I got to the office, two other kids were already in handcuffs with a sheriff watching over them. My soon to be co-defendants communicated to me with their eyes that we were in some deep shit. One of these idiots had dropped a half-ounce of marijuana on the ground during the rap cypher when we all broke out from the side of the building. Then the basketball coach went out to investigate and stumbled upon the sack of ganja. He recognized the three of us out of the crowd and reported the incident to the principal. Not only did we get suspended from school for three days, but we were also arrested for possession of marijuana. It was the first time I had felt the cold steel of handcuffs around my wrist. As the sheriff put us into his patrol car, I thought about how I was going to tell my parents that they would have to come to pick me up from jail. My father was at work, so I dared not to call him. My one phone call during booking would be to my mother at home. I sank into the back seat of the patrol car at the thought of having to tell her I was in the county jail.

Fortunately, that ordeal blew over with the charges being dropped; no one admitted to the weed being theirs, and it wasn't found on us or our property, so we were found not guilty of the possession of marijuana charge. Unfortunately, that would not be the last time I got suspended or arrested that school year. I was involved in several fights. One was with five guys that had jumped me because I was getting the best of their homeboy in a one on one fight. My threats to come back and shoot up the school didn't help my case. This made the principal believe I was in a gang, and they decided to expel me from the school district. My in and out of the courtroom left me with a year of supervised probation with anger management classes and community service. I broke it off with Serafina, who had been seeing some guy behind my back while I was grinding on the street corners. My parents had all but given up on me. I had let them down once again. Now that I had probation, it was their top priority to see me complete everything the law had assigned me to. My life was on the decline, and I didn't have a care about that in me.

My mother would have some tasks for me to do before she went to work in the afternoons: any and everything pertaining to her immaculate landscaping or bountiful garden. I would find myself up at the crack of dawn with a list of things she would have me do for both punishment and assistance to her.

If I played my cards right, I could get up and leave the house before she was up, leaving my day to hang out in the pool hall and serve crackheads, and write rhymes instead of the manual labor that awaited me at home. After a couple of hours of that, I couldn't wait for my homies to get out of school so they could fill me in on what I missed out on. Every week, I had to report to my probation officer and attend an anger management class. I dreaded both for serval reasons. The first being that the probation office and the anger management classes were in our rival town. My probation officer was this grimace of a White man who didn't necessarily want to see me make it off the probation sentence.

Appointments were sporadic and canceled without warning. Not to mention my sudden breakup with Mary Jane if I was going to pass the drug test. I knew her and I would have to go our separate ways for the time being. The anger management instructor was this gorgeous light-skinned woman who was very easy on the eyes, not so much on the ears. During her assessment, she would ask questions, trying to find the root of what I was angry about. I didn't have anger issues. I simply didn't give a fuck! I would say to myself as she picked and probed at my brain.

Chapter 12: Dope Stories

One Saturday morning, I decided to hit the block early. I made sure to re-up on crack before I snuck my way into the football game that Friday night. As usual, the game was followed up with a night of partying, so I missed out on all the crackheads getting paid and being more than ready to spend their hard-earned money on the little white devils they loved to smoke. My beeper was vibrating like crazy from the night before. I tried calling my customers back to no avail. Frustrated and unable to self-medicate, I decided to go uptown to the pool hall, where I could catch a few sales and get in a game or two of pool.

As soon as I turned the corner, I saw this older woman pacing back and forth in front of the hall. I didn't recognize her, and by the way she looked up at me, she didn't know me either. We both seemed to be contemplating over a mirrored thought. My thought was whether she wanted to buy some dope off of me? Hers appeared to be whether I had dope she could buy off of me? I proceeded into the pool hall with our questions unanswered, dropping in the right amount of quarters to play a solo game of pool. A minute or two passed, then she walked in and asked me for a cigarette. "Are you holding?" she finally asked after I answered no to her previous inquiry. I nodded yes and pointed toward the door.

Once outside, I noticed the woman had to be at least fifteen years my senior and was very attractive for a crack feind. "How much are you looking for?" I asked, looking her up and down. "A lot." She said, studying me as well. "My boyfriend will be back any minute now with the money." She said reassuringly. My dissatisfaction was written all over my face. "If your dope is good, we are going to spend money with you all day." She said, seeing if I would take the bait. I studied her more. Even though I didn't trust her, I wanted to believe that she would spend money with me all day. I needed that type of cash. "My dope is scutter!" I said, removing any doubt that she may have had after going back and forth with her for a minute. I took one of the twenty pieces of crack and broke it in half with my fingernail. "Here, try it for yourself." I said, placing the crack rock into her palm. The feind scurried in between the pool hall and my uncle's club, returning satisfied after testing my product. "It's good, baby!" she said in a relaxed tone. She came closer to me, suggesting that she pay for the hit with a blow job. I declined and told her I would rather have the money she planned to spend with me. "He should be back anytime now."

She said with her mouth screwed up in the usual crackhead way. I gave her my pager number, thinking to myself that with this lick, I should be sold out by two o'clock; and headed back home. About an hour later, the feind paged me from the payphone inside the pool hall. I darted back uptown in hopes no one had intercepted my cash cow.

"I just talked to my boyfriend, he said he was leaving in fifteen minutes." She said with a hint of annoyance in her voice. I gave her a head nod and took a seat at the counter. The woman came up behind me and asked if I could give her two rocks on credit until her boyfriend came. "That's sixty dollars." I said to remind the feind of her debt. "Oh, he's good for it." She said, scooping the crack out of my palm. "I'll page you again when he gets here." She assured me, walking out of the pool hall. I stepped outside to a buzzing sidewalk of people. It was already noon, and I had not made one single red cent. I needed to relax, and the only way I knew how was to roll a spliff, inhale the chronic smoke and blow out the bullshit. I had no concern about my P.O. violating me because of dirty piss. I made my way to the run-down apartments that were beside the pool hall and knocked on the door of apartment 4B. It belonged to another crackhead who was known to be a big-time drug dealer some thirty years ago. Everybody uptown used his place for their agenda. He had a spare room for "tricking" visitors. Some visitors used his kitchen to cook up dope. All types of fuckery took place in apartment 4B. I just needed a place to cop a bag of weed and smoke and not be too far from the pool hall when I got the page from the woman with the boyfriend.

"Come on in." The snaggle tooth man said when he opened the door. As I entered the small apartment, the pungent smell of reefer, crack, and mildew consumed my nostrils. There had to be at least twenty other hustlers gathered in the living room. I gave out a couple of head nods and daps as I made my way through the sea of dope dealers. "Damn, we got the whole Wu-Tang Clan up in this motherfucker!" a familiar voice said as they entered the apartment. It was my cousin Chris who had just come home from a five-year state prison sentence. Everyone was there waiting to buy dope from him. I let him handle his business and waited until the apartment cleared out. Chris had at least two grand to stuff into his pockets. "I see you shining big, cuz!" I said, lighting up a blunt I had rolled while waiting. "I didn't know you were holding weight?" I said while passing off the blunt to him. "Yes, cuz, more money in it than the hand to hand grind."

Chris said while racking the crumbs of crack cocaine off a plate into the tenant's hands. "I didn't know you were slanging rocks." He then said, passing the blunt back to me. We sat and smoked another blunt and talked before leaving the apartment, making plans to hook back up later to visit two girls he knew in a neighboring city. I checked my beeper, scrolling through the history, and there were no recent pages. "I gotta go back to the pool hall real quick. Come to the crib. I'll be ready in an hour." I said as Chris and I went our separate ways.

When I made it back to the pool hall, the woman and her boyfriend were nowhere in sight. I asked a couple of people if they had seen the woman, and unanimously, none of the patrons had seen her since earlier. I'll deal with this later, I thought, kicking myself for not being diligent in my dealings with this crack feind. I decided to go home and get ready for my plans with Chris. When Chris and I got back from seeing the girls, it was much later than I had anticipated. We laughed and joked about the chicks and their antics on the ride back to our town. I had a lot of fun, but in the back of my mind was unfinished business. I had Chris drop me off in front of the pool hall. I walked around the block a couple of times in hopes of running into the woman and her boyfriend. I eventually bumped into Cederio, who had been looking for Chris to re-up. "Where y'all been at?" He said discouraged. "Fucking with some broads Chris knew. Hey, have you seen this new crackhead lady?" "About this high, pretty face, big ass titties?" I said, just as discouraged as Cederio was. "You mean the 'trick,' she been trying to sell pussy all day up here, yea, man, I just passed her, What's up?" When I filled him in on what had happened, Cederio wanted to help me find her and get my money, or at least him, and I would take turns fucking her until she paid off her sixty dollar debt to me. After an hour or so, we finally found somebody that knew where the woman was, but they hadn't seen any guy that could be her boyfriend with her.

I could feel my blood boil as I replayed that morning's events over in my mind. This bitch had no intentions of paying me my money. There probably wasn't a boyfriend, and she knew the only way she could pay for her crack fix was by sucking and fucking for it. "Motherfucker." I mumbled to myself as Cederio and I made our way up the hill to where we were told she was last seen. "When you get inside, make sure you let her know she fucked up." Cederio said in a coaching way. "Um huh." I said, tightlipped. "You might have to slap her around a little." He said as we made it to the front door of the house.

I snatched at the screen door and found the front door was open. Cederio and I invited ourselves into the house. "What the fuck!?" the tenant yelled, shocked and surprised by the two of us standing in his living room. There she was, the woman who thought she had got away with hustling me. No longer did she look attractive as she had earlier. Her hair was out of place, and her makeup was smeared. Her eyes were bulging and bloodshot. She was almost naked as she sat there with a crack pipe in hand. She was looking as if she had seen a ghost. As I took in my surroundings, I felt my hand clench into a fist, and before I knew it, I threw jab after jab into this woman's face. The first punch struck her eye, and it swelled immediately. She dropped the crack pipe right as the second punch landed on her jaw. The third and fourth punch drew blood from her now swollen face, then a mist of blood sprayed onto the window curtain. The woman grabbed her face finally and let out a scream so loud it took me out of my violent trance. "Yo! We gotta get the fuck outta here!" Cederio said, grabbing my arm and leading me out of the crime scene. We ran toward the pool hall, taking the alley to find a place to lay low. "Damn man, I told you to slap her around not to beat her face in." Cederio said, almost out of breath. By the time we found a place to keep me out of sight, police cars began circling the block. This wasn't unusual, but we both knew they could be looking for whoever had given the woman the beating of her life. "Stay here. I'm going to go check it out and see what's happening." Cederio said, still looking in the direction of the police car. "Ight ..." I finally managed to say as he walked back uptown.

As I sat alone in the darkness, I thought about what I had done to that woman's face. I tried to justify my fit of anger by thinking she was just a crackhead. I had no respect or remorse for crackheads. I still couldn't shake the images of her face and blood that played over and over in my head. Cederio came back after a while and told me that the woman was talking to the police and that she told them that her boyfriend was the one that had abused her, that he had caught her with her lover and was outraged by her cheating. We stayed in our hideout long enough to smoke a blunt before we would head home. "Her boyfriend's name is cocaine. He been beating her ass." He said with a laugh. I mustered up a whimper of a laugh as I massaged my tender bloodstained knuckles.

Chapter 13: Menace

As the spring of '96 came in, I found myself unable to get away from the house and avoid the manual labor my mother would have me to do. One day I was trimming the hedges when an unfamiliar car drove up into our driveway. When the driver stepped out, I was surprised to see my old English teacher, Ms. Howard. "Ms. Howard!?" I asked as if it wasn't obvious. "Hi...is your mother home?" She asked as she made her way to where I stood in the front yard. I was taken aback as to why she was there. "Yes, ma'am, she's in the house." I said, pausing "Who Shot Ya?" By the Notorious B.I.G. on my Walkman.

After all the trouble I had found myself in while I was in school, my expulsion would make it where I couldn't return to any school in the county or surrounding counties. I was labeled as a menace, so Ms. Howard's presence had me baffled. I watched as the middle-aged White woman carrying several folders was greeted by my mother when she reached the door. The two of them disappeared into the house. I usually dragged when it came to my chores, but that day I finished the yard work in record time. When I walked into the house, I saw Ms. Howard and my mother both smiling as they looked over some paperwork at our dining room table. My curiosity was getting the best of me. What in the world could they be talking about?

"Come here for a second." My mother instructed, pulling out a chair for me. "Ms. Howard has something she would like to discuss with us." I took my seat between the two of them, wondering what kind of trouble could I be in now. "Well...your mother and I are aware of how intelligent you are." Ms. Howard said as she slid some test scores in front of me. "In my class, you aced every test, and your participation was better than most. I have to admit you were one of my favorite students." She said, grinning at my mother. "Your mother and I agree you have too much potential to go to waste. I've had talks with the Board of Education on your behalf to have them reconsider allowing you back into school based on your academic record." I looked at Ms. Howard and then my mother as she continued explaining. "They denied your re-entry for the remainder of the school year. However, they did offer you the chance to finish the eleventh grade if you were to be homeschooled by an accredited instructor." Ms. Howard paused, searching for a reaction on my face. My mother was searching for the same thing as they gave me a collective blank stare. "I was more than glad to volunteer for the job...isn't that great?" She asked, giving me her biggest smile. I didn't know what to think as I had gotten used to not being in school and dealing with tests and homework. Having time to sell dope and write rhymes and smoke weed had become my daily routine. I did miss the girls and my homies at school though. "This is only going to work if you are committed to doing the work." My mother chimed into the conversation. "You need to take advantage of this. Ms. Howard and I know you can do it, but you have to want to do it." I stared at my mom as her words lingered in the air. This was the first time in a long time I felt awful and remorseful for my actions. How embarrassed she must have been to have to come and bail me out of jail those times. I deserved to look into my mother's eyes and feel like I had let her down. On the contrary, she did not deserve to look at me and feel she had let me down. "Ok, I want to do this!" I said to them, surprising myself with my answer. They both let out a sigh of relief. We discussed the details of my homeschooling and planned to start my first lesson the following week. I couldn't help but give Ms. Howard a hug as I said goodbye. "Thank you, Ms. Howard. I appreciate what you're doing for me." She flashed her famous big smile at me. "You are very much welcome, young man."

By the time summer came around, my schedule now consisted of selling dope by day and homeschooling at the local library with Ms. Howard in the afternoon. I still had the anger management classes twice a week and visitations with my probation officer. On my last visit to the probation office, my urine tested positive for THC. The only reason my P.O. didn't violate me was that I had started homeschooling and had attended all of my anger management classes up to that point, so he gave me one final chance to pass the urine test. I had to stop smoking pot. There was no way to avoid the break.

The one on one learning with Ms. Howard started off boring at first, but it didn't take long for us to get into the swing of things. We breezed through lesson after lesson, quiz after quiz, and test after test on all the subjects required of me to complete the eleventh grade. I found myself wanting to study all the time, especially on topics that weren't in my textbooks.

My parents had collections of books on Black history in America. These piqued my interest, and I began to study these along with my course material. With only a month or so left before school would start up again, my summer had been absent of the one thing all teenage boys earnestly sought out during the hot months, a girl. "Yo, what time are you gonna be done at the library?" Drake asked me on one of his visits. "Usually about 4:30 PM. What's up? I replied as I packed my bag for that day's lessons. "Oh ok, I got something for ya, cuz!" he said with a grin. I returned a grin at him. What Drake had for me could be only one or two things. Money or a girl. "My girl got a homegirl who is trying to meet you later. We are going to go to Pizza Hut around seven o'clock, you down?" he asked, already knowing the answer to his question. This would be his and his girlfriend's third attempt at hooking me up with one of her friends. The first two were not my type or what I was used to dating, so I was a little skeptical. "Man, I'm down." I said, thinking the third time's the charm.

After my studies at the library were done for the day, I went back to my house to get ready for my date. While in the shower, I could hear my beeper vibrating on the bathroom countertop. Without looking, I knew those were customers looking to spend some money. There was no time for me to get dressed, head uptown, serve the crackheads, and be in place at 6:00 p.m. I tried calling Drake at our grandfather's house but didn't get an answer. "I gotta get this paper!" I said as I left the house for uptown. It wasn't long before I had made a quick two hundred and fifty dollars. Looking at the time on my beeper, it was already after six. I knew Drake and his girlfriend would come looking for me uptown, so I decided to stay put and wait for them there. After a game of pool, I stepped out into the warm summer evening and lit up a Black & Mild, trying to calm my nerves with the rich tobacco smoke. Just then, a burgundy and silver Nissan Maxima pulled up in front of the pool hall.

"We been looking for you, cuz, should have known you would be up here." Drake said from the passenger seat. I put out the miniature cigar and secretly sprayed Joop Cologne on my shirt, popped some Tic Tacs into my mouth, and headed to the rear of the car. As I pulled the door handle, my eyes met with the eyes of my date. My coolness was lost on her. She was beautiful and held a striking resemblance to Sasha, whom I had admired as a freshman. Her mahogany skin tone poked out from behind a mid-cut hairdo. She had very little makeup, so her beauty was all hers. I slid into the backseat of the car, next to the lovely stranger, inhaling her fragrance. "You can stop looking all sad now, Mona. We found him." Drake said teasingly. "Shut up." She retorted, half smiling. "Hey, Mona. Nice to meet you finally."

I said, taking her hand into mine and giving it a peck of a kiss. Drake laughed hysterically from the front seat. The four of us chatted all the way to our destination. "So...are you a bad boy trying to be good or a good boy trying to be bad?" Mona asked me as we ate our pizza. "All of the above." I said, laying on my player persona pretty thick. "I hope all of me is welcomed." She looked deeply into my eyes as I told her stories of my adventures in the street.

After we ate, we decided to head over to the city park. Drake wanted to smoke a blunt, and his girlfriend wouldn't allow him to smoke it in the car. Mona watched me closely as I blew Drake a shotgun. The strong reefer smoke caused him to cough, which caused me to laugh until I was interrupted by my beeper going off again. I disregarded the incoming pages, putting the device into silent mode. Mona gave me a wink when I looked up at her. She loved the fact that I was a dope dealing, gun-toting rapper with chestnut-colored eyes, so much that we exchanged numbers by the end of the night. At this point, I hadn't the slightest idea that in the years to come, Mona and I would be married.

Needless to say, we hit it off. By the end of the summer, Mona and I had become a couple. On the days I was scheduled to see my P.O. or attend anger management class, I would walk the few blocks over to her house. I had met her mom, and she had met my parents as well. We were in love. I found myself spending more and more time with her and less and less time hustling and hanging out with my homies. "Oh, baby, you didn't have to do this!" Mona said, gushing all over herself when I brought in several bags of clothes for her during a visit. "I know, but you're my girl. If I'm fly, you gotta be fly!" I said with sarcasm. She laughed and smiled from ear to ear as she held up random clothing against her body. "I love you, boy!" She said, kissing me and hugging my neck tightly.

My lessons at the library with Ms. Howard had ended, and I received all my class credits passing the eleventh grade with an A average. In the coming school year, I would be a senior. My outlook on my future was changing. I knew that I couldn't sell dope forever. I started to feel ashamed about the poison I was selling to people that looked like me. It was genocide. The African American books I would study left me with a sense of pride and accomplishment. When I came across the Autobiography of Malcolm X, something clicked in my brain. A light switch was thrown on. In him, I saw myself. His Detroit Red persona related to me now some thirty years after he had become one of the greatest Black minds in American history. The book would be the catalyst for the change that was stirring inside of me. I hadn't put any thought into what it was I wanted to be, as the saying went when I grew up. As I began thinking about the answer to the proverbial question, I realized I wanted to make a difference and to do that, I had to do things differently. I had spent the last eight years trying to make a name for myself; trying to be better than a Kenny Southerland; trying to get from under the shadow of my dad and my brother; trying to keep the Grim Reaper at bay. Those efforts brought on some uncomfortable situations for my family and me. The life I had been living was a 360-degree rotation of lust, greed, and violence, if not all the other four deadly sins. I had spun out of control. I made up my mind then, and there it was time for a 180-degree change in the right direction.

Chapter 14: My Inspiration

Being in the graduating class of '97 was rewarding from the very start. For me, it was surreal. I hadn't thought about graduating from high school since I was in junior high. I took advantage of every elective, club, or function that I possibly could. I was still the popular cool kid my classmates remembered, but it wouldn't be long for them and others to notice the change within me. Long gone were the days of skipping class and being high or drunk in the hallway. Now it was all about academics. English class had been my favorite subject since elementary. Thanks to a thirty-something year old White stuntwoman who knew her way around Tinseltown, this was about to change. Her name was Ms. Brock, and on the first day of theatre, we both seemed to be unimpressed. I was one of two seniors in the class. The rest of the class was made up of underclassmen. A mixed bag of outcasts, geeks, and nerds. "Ok, class, today we will be practicing the art of improvisation." She said, looking as if she was reconsidering her career path. She began to scribble something on index cards. "You will, on cue, act out whatever animal is printed on the index card." I sat on the stage and looked onward as my classmates gave their best impressions of a bird, a lion, and an elephant. When it was my turn to take center stage, I received the index card with a monkey scribbled on it. I immediately contoured my body to mimic an orangutan making my arms appear longer than normal, waving them about over my head as I monkey walked across the center stage. Ms. Brock and the rest of the class broke out into a burst of laughter as I got more into character. As I paraded around, walking on my knuckles and belting out loud screeching sounds, Ms. Brock's face lit up in delight. I swung on my hands and flipped over to where she sat and proceeded to pick through her hair, picking and eating imaginary bugs from it. The theater roared with laughter and clapping as my performance came to an end. Ms. Brock rose to her feet and said, "Now, class, that's what you call an improv!"

Mona had called me up one day and said she thought she was pregnant. After taking a couple of pregnancy tests, it was confirmed that she was indeed pregnant. We decided not to have an abortion. For the moment, we were able to hide her pregnancy until we figured out how and when we would tell our parents. Our relationship was going great, and the thought of us being a mother and father in a couple of months didn't put a damper on our love for one another. If anything, it made it that much stronger. I finally acquired my driver's license, which was no small feat. First I had to convince my mom and dad that I would be a responsible driver. Then there was the written and driving test. I learned how to drive on my own back when my cousin Kaiden and I had bought the hooptie. Still, my parents thought I should take some formal instruction, and they recruited my brother Vick to instruct. "Ok, now push the clutch in with your left foot and ease off the break with your right as you shift into third gear." Vick said as I was already one step ahead of his command. "Hey, bro, you are a natural!" He said as I accelerated to the speed limit. Beaming with pride, I turned the radio on just in time to catch Jodeci's "Feenin'" fade into a commercial break.

"So, how's your senior year of high school so far?" My brother asked as if that wasn't what he wanted to ask me. "It's cool. I'm glad to be back in school this year!" I said, checking the speedometer as we cruised along the highway. "Oh, ok, have you uhhhh...started having uh...sex yet?" he asked in the most awkward of tone. I looked over at him and thought for a second. Had my brother been a spy planted by my parents? Or was he being a big brother? I rolled the dice. "Yeah, would you like some tips on techniques?" We burst into uncontrollable laughter that sabotaged his talk about the birds and bees, skipping right to the discussion about the dogs and the cats.

Even though I had cleaned up my act and began to make plans for the future, I would still entertain certain habits. One being my love for smoking weed. After school, my house had become the "hangout" spot for my brethren and me. We would chill and smoke up until my father would come from work. By now, I had completed probation and the anger management classes. One day, Mona called and said she and Drake's girlfriend were coming over. I told her I would be there, happy that I would get the chance to see her before the weekend. My crew and I sat on the front porch of my house, smoking and talking like we usually did when Mona pulled up into the driveway in her mother's car. She had only obtained her license a day before. "Hey, baby!" I yelled in her direction as the two of them got out of the car. As we finished up the spliff that was in rotation, the girls joined us on the porch. After a while, the house phone rang, and I excused myself to answer it. When I returned outside moments later, I was greeted with a hard slap to the face by Mona. As stunned as I was, the ringing in my ear subsided to the snickering of my homeboys.

I could feel the anger rise from deep down inside of me, clawing its way up from the shallow grave I had buried it in weeks before in anger management class. The logical side of my brain was trying to compute why the mother of my unborn child had slapped me. My heart rate was up, pounding in my chest like a war drum. As these things took place internally, externally, I was calm and frozen in place. Mona broke out into tears and ran back to her mother's car and locked all the doors. Her tears were sobering, and I was able to move again and found myself at the driver's side of the vehicle. "Are you ok. What's wrong?" Was all I could muster out of all the confusion going on in my heart and my mind. I didn't even acknowledge the burst of laughter coming from my friends behind me. "I'm ready to go!" Mona said, ignoring my presence and pledging for her to stay and talk it out. As the car pulled out of the driveway, my head hung low as I made my way back to the front porch. My crew shook their collective heads at the situation. I later learned through Drake that the reason behind the slap was a dare of sorts while I was in the house answering the phone. Mona felt the need to tell my friends how she had me wrapped around her finger. Of course, they felt the need to tell her I wasn't wrapped too tight in the head, and there was no way I would go for anything like that. The "dare" was if she were to slap me that I would most certainly hit her back, at the least. The fact that I didn't even raise my voice, let alone lay a hand on her, baffled my homies. It did give Mona the impression that she did have me wrapped around her finger. Up until that incident, there had been no incidents that would blemish our teenage love. Even though it was quickly resolved, it would be evidence of things to come.

As the weeks flew by, Mona's body started going through the changes. For a sixteen-year-old girl, it was a horrific time. Her clothes no longer fit properly, then there was the morning sickness and the cravings for food and sex. I did what I could to accommodate her. We had put off telling her mother as long as we could, but now four months into the pregnancy, she needed prenatal care. When we finally decided to tell her mother, she said she already knew. "Y'all think I'm dumb or something?" Were her exact words.

My parents weren't surprised either. I think they were somewhat glad about the news. They liked Mona. To them, she seemed to be my inspiration for slowing down and leaving the streets alone. "We will be glad to help out with the baby!" my parents said, gushing at the news about their grandchild. As two teenage parents, I can honestly say the odds of success were not against us. This baby that was due in six months was becoming an answer and not a problem.

My grades were the best they had ever been. If I weren't studying a school subject, I had my nose in some book about African American history. I was researching the likes of Marcus Garvey or Sojourner Truth. Those stories inspired me to be the best or make the best out of the worst situations. I had now found pride in my Black skin. In drama class, I would get the lead character in every school production we put on. The more plays we did, the more people attended. My popularity and acting prowess made the drama club a cool thing to be a part of. I was riding high. It seemed that anything I applied myself to, I became successful in it. "You have this great talent!" Ms. Brock said as I finished my monologue of Scrooge in a Christmas Carol. "Thanks, Ms. Brock. Your advice is helping." I said, returning the encouragement. "I wanted to tell you that at last week's opening, there was a write up in the newspaper. There were some important people in the audience that night." Ms. Brock said while we walked backstage. "Important people like who?" I said, grinning from ear to ear. "People that would like to see you take your acting as far as possible!" She said, holding up my accepted application for the state regional drama competition. I rushed Ms. Brock and gave her a huge hug. "This could mean a college scholarship for you, and I'm so proud!" she said, holding back a tear.

"Thank you so much Ms. Brock. I won't let you down." I said conformingly. "You damn right, you won't! She said, wiping away a tear. "Now get out of here. You're ruining my makeup."

Under the guidance of Ms. Brock, another classmate and I took the competition by storm. There was another write up in the newspaper, and we received all types of accolades from the school. During Black History Month, I was asked to do a piece for the Black History program my school was doing that year. I would have full creative control over it. I knew I would portray Malcolm X. One day, I was walking into the library and bumped into Kia. Even though I would see her around, we hardly ever talked anymore. "Fancy bumping into you today." She said, giggling. "Yea, no kidding." I said with a grin. "You got a minute?" I asked, almost pleading. "Yes, I'm working in the library this period. What's up?' She said, surprised at my request after all this time. "I wanted to apologize for—" She interrupted. "I know. All has been forgiven." I interrupted her back, "It's just that you were right about a lot of things. I had to learn the hard way." I went on like that for most of the conversation, telling her about Mona and the baby and how I still thought about her from time to time. She made it easy for me to end my rambling. Somehow, she decrypted what I was saying and ended our conversation by saying, "I still love you too." Then walked away.

I left the library shortly after and headed to my next period class when I caught Ms. Howard going into her classroom. "Hey, Ms. Howard. How are you?" I said excitedly. "Well, just the guy I wanted to see." She said. "You were looking for me?" I asked, puzzled. "Yes, I have some great news." She paused for a second to gather her thoughts and lesson planner, then looked up at the clock, then at me. "Oh, I'll just write you a pass to your next class." She finally said. "Have you ever heard of the Ellman scholarship?" I gave her a blank stare, telling her that I had not. "Well, it's a scholarship that they give to only one student per school year, and you meet the criteria of having made the most significant changes over the past year. "Oh, wow. So what all do I have to do?" I asked eagerly. "You have to write a five hundred and fifty word essay, explaining how you changed for the better and why. I think you can handle that?" She said mockingly, knowing that writing was my strong suit. "Of course, Ms. Howard!" I said, mocking her as well. She handed me the application for the scholarship and a hall pass. "Be sure to return this to me before the deadline and tell your mother I said hello." She said with her usual grin. I turned to leave, reading over the application. "I will, Ms. Howard." I said with confidence. "I'm proud of you, young man!" I smiled at her and headed off to my next class. As I walked and read the scholarship details, my jaw dropped when I read the line about the twenty thousand dollars, and this would provide to the college of my choice. Here I had two chances at scholarships and had not even taken the SAT.

Chapter 15: Damage Control

Mona had a doctor's appointment that afternoon, so I borrowed my dad's car to take her. At this particular appointment, we would find out the sex of the baby. As always, she was hungry and horny. The combination worked for me, as well. When we made it to the health clinic, we had to wait a while to be seen. Mona drummed up a conversation about her ex-boyfriend trying to rekindle with her. "So, what did you tell him?" I asked, trying to sound nonchalant. "I told him that I was having your baby, that we were getting married, that he had his chance before, and now it's too late." Mona's ex was this knucklehead who was locked up in the county jail. He would have somebody call her on three-way, so she would answer his calls. She assured me over and over that he wasn't a threat. I had never considered any guy a "threat" when I was with a girl. My confidence or conceitedness wouldn't allow the thought to anchor down in my mind. "Oh, ok. I might have to see that nigga when he gets out!" I said, playing into my tuff side that Mona loved so much. I leaned in and gave her a peck on the lips. "It must be something in the air. I talked to my ex Kia today at school, and she told me she still loved me." I said innocently. "Oh, did she now?" Mona retorted in her usual angry Black girl manner. "Yea, it's ok though. I told her about you and the baby, and she was happy for me." I said reassuringly. Her beautiful face was contoured in a way that let me know she wasn't assured at all. "You can come back now." The nurse finally said, not realizing she had saved me from trouble with her patient. As I sat there and watched the nurse take Mona's vital signs and then set up equipment for the ultrasound, my anticipation grew with each movement the nurse made. In moments, I would see the baby and learn if it was a boy or a girl. I had already picked out names based on sex. If the baby was a boy, we would name him Tye, and if it was a girl, we would name her Dosia. I had lifted the names from a Smif N Wessun freestyle rap, where they had referenced their love of marijuana. "It looks like you guys are having a little girl." The nurse said, smiling at the discovery. "I told you so!" Mona said, smiling at me at her prediction coming true. "I'm happy either way love!" I said. We both stared at the tiny monitor in amazement, looking at our creation. It was a glimpse into the future for me. All my dreams of success now had a successor. My daughter had become my muse. I was giving a hundred percent into my endeavors. From that day on, I would give it a hundred fifty.

"That's a dope name, homey!" Kaiden said to me as we sat in the studio, waiting for the engineer to set up so we could begin our recording session. "General Steele killed the verse, right?" I asked my rhyme partner as I rolled a blunt. "No doubt, so who's your baby's mom?" Kaiden asked while looking through a crate of records. "She goes to school out here. You went to school out here at some point, right?" I asked, lighting up the blunt. "You might know her, Mona Anderson?" I asked while taking a final tote before passing it off to him. "Yea, I know shorty. I tried to holla at her back in the day." He said, retrieving the blunt from me. "Man, what girl haven't you tried to holla at son!?" I asked rhetorically. "Damn, if I know!" He said with his lungs full of chronic smoke. We laughed at the irony of it all. "You got a bad one though son!" Kaiden said, passing the spliff back to me. Just then, the engineer walked into the room. "Y'all ready?" he asked, holding his breath, trying not to catch a contact. We nodded to him that we were and clipped the half-smoked cigar. We were indeed ready. This session would be the first since we took our music careers into our own hands. The label we were signed to wasn't making things happen as fast as we would have liked them to. I had a hookup with the DJ that spun records at the local radio station and skating rink. He guaranteed me he would play our single after he heard our street buzz. The thing was we didn't have a single. The label had the rights to all the music we recorded under them. That would all change by the end of the night. It only took us two takes to lay down a catchy hook and another for both our verses. The engineer produced the beat, and the blunt we smoked earlier gave us the mojo to bring it. Two hours later, we had our single.

We left the studio that night feeling ourselves. We listened to the track over and over again in the car on the way back home. "Yo, I'm going to take the edited clean version to the radio station tomorrow." I said, nodding my head to the infectious bassline. "Ight, cool, let me know, and I'll meet you up there." Kaiden said, extending his hand to me to do our signature handshake. As he backed out of the driveway, he yelled out, "Shit is too hot!" as he started the track over again. I laughed and nodded in agreeance. As I walked up to my house, I looked up at the night sky. The stars were intensely bright against the dark sky backdrop. I couldn't help but feel like one of those stars. I tingled from head to toe, pausing for a moment, realizing how everything was going in my favor. "Oh God, thank you for this!" I said as I stared up in the heavens. I had a big day ahead of me. Mona and I were going out to eat in celebration of our little girl. Kaiden and I would be debuting our first single on the radio later that night. I was still practicing my speech for the Black

History program, not to mention the scholarship essay. I was tired, and I loved it. It meant that I was accomplishing things. Now I was able to get some rest but not before listening to our single one last time.

Waking up on a Saturday morning with a full itinerary always gave me an electrifying sense of worth. First, I was off to the Brewer Brothers for a fresh haircut but not before calling Mona to make sure she would be ready when I arrived. The Brewer Brothers back porch was as it always was on a Saturday morning. Red plastic cups filled with liquor and White Owl or Philly blunts rolled up with the chronic. I took mine in moderation, not wanting to get too fucked up too early. After getting my haircut and leaving with an ok buzz, I headed home to shower and get dressed and to call Mona yet again, pleading her to be ready when I got there. I anticipated her not being prepared when I pulled up to her house an hour later.

As I waited, her little brother and I got in a game of Tecmo Bowl, and I had a chance to test our song out on him. As we played the video game, I borrowed Mona's radio and played the tape for him, not telling him it was me to get his real reaction. He nodded along with the beat, and after playing it a couple more times, he began singing along with the hook. By halftime, I was up a touchdown, and Mona was finally out of the bathroom. "Hey, baby, I'm almost ready." She said, peeking into her brother's room. "What's that song you keep playing over and over? It's hot!" "That's our song. I'm taking it to the radio station today if my baby mama would hurry up." I said, grilling her brother because he scored a touchdown while I wasn't paying attention. "That's your song!?" She said, running into her brother's room. "My baby daddy is going to be famous!"

We finally made it to our favorite eatery and ate until we had our fill. We took our time at the table and discussed the baby, school, and then out of nowhere. "So, what did your ex-girlfriend say to you again?" Mona asked in a faux calm voice. "What? I already told you what she said." I replied, mirroring her tone. "Uh huh...but you didn't tell me what you said." She said with her usual attitude. I looked at the mother of my child as if she had two heads. Obviously, one of them had lost their mind. I knew most of this was due to the pregnancy with her emotions rollercoastering all over the place. I wanted her to relax and trust me. So, as I explained Kia's and my conversation to her again, I did my best to consider her feelings. We left the restaurant shortly after and headed over to the radio station. She was as quiet as a mouse pissing on a piece of cotton on the ride over. I tried to make her laugh and get her mind off of Kia with not much luck. "I'll be right back." I told her while getting out of the car and noticing her still sulking and pouting.

Once inside of the radio station, my mind was strictly on getting our single played. I will deal with Mona later, I thought. The DJ greeted me, and I followed him into the program manager's office. He took the tape of our single and played it, making sure the editing and quality were up to par. "Yo, y'all got a banger right here fam!" he said as he nodded his head along with the drumline. I nodded along with him. "Yea, I know!" I said, feeling very enthusiastic now about the track. "Alright, you guys be back here around 6:30 PM tonight. My show starts at 7:00 PM ok?" he said more as a statement than a question. "Mind if I hold on to the tape?" "No, not at all...we will be here!" I said, assuring him we wouldn't miss the opportunity.

I ran down the steps and back to the car, super excited at the news. "I have great news, babe. The DJ loves the song and wants to interview us tonight on his Top 7 at 7 broadcast! Isn't that great?" I said, holding in my excitement as best as

I could. Mona looked at me with a stare that felt like a laser cutting me in half. "So, that means our day is pretty much over?" she said, now aiming her laser directly at the middle of my forehead. "Well...I mean...I'll make it up to you babe. I promise." I said, searching for the right words to say so that I wouldn't enrage her further. "Take me home." She retorted, shifting her tone from angry to disappointed.

On the drive back to her house, we were both quiet. I would glance over at her as she stared out the passenger window. I was thinking about the song and the interview and what that meant for our music careers. I had no idea what Mona was conjuring up in her head. She broke the silence by asking me, "Isn't that where Kia lives?" "Yep, she lives out there." I said sheepishly. "Let's go to her house." She said, more demanding than asking. "Hell, nah. For what? I already told you everything!" "If you have nothing to hide, what's the problem?" She said with her face showing a trace of suspicion. "I just want to talk to her to see if you are telling me the truth." "I'm telling you the truth!" I rebutted. "Prove it." She said, boxing me into a moral corner. I shook my head and turned into Kia's subdivision. I thought of all the possible scenarios that could play out. Mona and Kia being face to face couldn't be that bad of a thing, right? I asked myself as I turned onto Kia's street.

I was relieved to see that Kia's mother's car wasn't there. "Doesn't look like they're home." I said, offering a chance to forget the whole thing. "I'll go ring the doorbell. Pull over." Mona countered. I pulled over in front of Kia's house and let out a long sigh. Just then, Kia's younger brother rode up in the yard on his bicycle. "Hey, is Kia home?" Mona asked in the most pleasant voice she could muster. "Yea, she's home. Let me get her for you." The kid said and ran inside to get his sibling. I knew Kia wasn't the type to start a fight or even an argument for that matter. If anything, I was worried that Kia might relay Mona's wrong ideas by being too honest about our conversation. It wasn't long before Kia came out to meet us. I studied both of them as I sat in the car. They both seemed at ease when Kia looked over at the car. I waved at her, feeling and looking like a real schmuck. Kia came over to the vehicle as Mona opened the car door and stepped out. I got out reluctantly, knowing I had to do some serious damage control now and later. "So, what is it you wanted to talk about?" Kia asked. It was plain to see she felt awkward from our impromptu visit. "What was it you and my man were talking about the other day at your school?" Mona asked with an attitude that was so ghetto. Kia looked over at me for a second, searching for some clue as to what to say. "I already told you." I said, trying to gain control over their conversation and the situation I found myself in. "I asked her!" Mona said, snapping at me.

Kia tried her best to lighten the mood. "Oh, in the library, yea, we talked about you guys. He told me about the baby, and I let him know that I was proud of him." She said with a hint of laughter. Kia didn't want to say what could have been taken out of context. She was protecting me and trying to preserve any integrity we had left in our dealings. "You think this is funny, bitch?" Mona yelled as she grabbed Kia by her hair and slammed her headfirst into the hood of the car. I was paralyzed for a second, which felt like an hour. "What the fuck is wrong with you?" I yelled in their direction, making my way to the other side of the car. My thoughts dashed about between the welfare of Mona, then the baby. Kia wasn't fighting back as Mona punched her repeatedly in the face. I was able to separate them after a moment of trying not to hurt either one of them. Kia fell on the pavement as a result. I ran over to her and asked if she was ok. She looked up at me with her eyes full of tears that had not yet fallen. I tried to help her up, but she rejected my hand. In the background Mona whimpered, "You're asking her if she's ok? What about me!?" Kia picked herself up off the sidewalk and brushed herself off and walked toward her house. I called to her in hopes of a response. Her silence said it all. She was hurt physically by Mona, but I had hurt her emotionally. She would not give either one of us the satisfaction of seeing her cry. Mona held her hand to her face and began to cry. This to me, was an insult to my already bruised heart and pride, if not my ego. She had caused this with her unwarranted insecurities and jealousy and dared to be playing the victim. "What the fuck are you crying for!" I asked, not caring for an answer. "Get in the fucking car!" I barked at her like a rabid junkyard dog. As Mona got into the passenger side of the car, I slammed the car door behind her.

Chapter 16: Local Celebrities

As I tore out of the subdivision back onto the highway, I could feel the surge of tension rise up from my calf muscles and up to the top of my spine. I started to floor the gas pedal, driving at speeds that exceeded the speed limit. Mona gave pause to her crying act as I swerved from one side of the road to the other, yelling at the top of my lungs. Her eyes widened as I lost complete control of myself, screaming at her how she had put herself and the baby in danger. Somehow, I kept control of the car. Mona worked up enough nerve to say that I was scaring her. "Shut the fuck up!" I said as I smashed the brake pedal with my foot, causing the car to come to a brief stop then fishtailing on to the side of the highway. Mona cradled her face in her hands, rocking back and forth, sobbing uncontrollably. I snatched at the door handle and let myself out. Now cursing to myself as I paced back and forth on the side of the highway, my heart was pounding, punching from the inside of my chest. I continued to pace until I had calmed down enough to go back to the car. I climbed back into the driver's seat, the key was still in the ignition, and everything was still running smoothly.

Mona sat holding her stomach, unable to look at me. Her makeup was ruined from all the crying, and her hair lay out of place. "I swear to God, if you ever pull some shit like that again, it's over between us." I said in a semi-calm voice. She didn't respond and continued to avoid making eye contact with me. I put the car in drive and turned back onto the highway. Both of us sat silent for the rest of the ride.

When I pulled up to her house and into the driveway, Mona got out of the car without saying a word. I drove off as soon as she closed the car door, not waiting like I usually would until she got inside the house. I had a little over an hour to be back at the radio station, so I pulled over at a corner store and used the payphone to call Kaiden, letting him know about the interview. As I made my way back over to the radio station, the fight between Mona and Kia played over and over in my mind. I knew that this was far from being over. Once I pulled into the radio station's parking lot, I noticed Kaiden was already there waiting for me. He was just as excited as I had been before the fight. "Peace, Peace, fam!" I said, extending my hand for a dap. "Yo, tell me you got some bud." "Of course. I just rolled up right before you pulled in." He said, reviving the Dutch Master he had behind his ear. We sat in the parking lot until we had smoked half of the spliff.

As my high settled in, I began to focus on the interview and the debut of our single. We made our way into the building and up the stairs to the studio door. Before Kaiden could knock, the DJ opened the door and greeted us inside. I was impressed right away by all the equipment, microphones, records, and multi-colored wires. I felt like I was at the pearly gates of heaven, and this was judgment day. "Glad you made it back on time. We have about ten minutes before we go live. Let me explain how we do the show." Kaiden and I listened as the engineer adjusted the big chrome microphones in front of us. Minutes later, the engineer flipped on the on the air from the control room. The DJ came to life like an animatronic fortune teller machine at a carnival. He spoke familiar words into his microphone that Kaiden and I had heard every Saturday night at seven o'clock. "You are now locked into the Top 7 at 7, where we play the hottest Hip Hop and RnB!" We looked at each other and nodded our heads in approval. "Tonight, we have a hot new single from our special guest! Y'all keep it locked in as we get the party going with a Mary J. Blige 'I'm Going Down (Remix)."

The DJ played song after song until he finally started the interview part of his broadcast. He introduced us and asked us questions about the group, our influences, and the respected hoods we represented. Finally, he played our single and went into a commercial break. The anticipation of the feedback from the listeners was unbearable. Kaiden and I held our breaths as we stared at the phone lines that sat about the studio. A couple of minutes went by as one of the phone lines began to ring. Then another one lit up and another and another. The DJ began answering the phones one by one.

"Sure, I can get that on for you." He said on one phone. "Yea, that's the bomb, right!" He said in another. I was about to explode like a bomb. What are they saying? I thought as I squirmed about in my chair. The DJ held up a finger at us, asking for a moment. Before long, all the phone lines were clear again. The DJ was poker-faced as he signaled over to the control room. Kaiden broke his silence. "So, do they like our song?"

"Do they! I had to route calls to the engineer so we could finish the countdown. There were so many requests to play it again!" the DJ said. "Check this out." He cued up the recording of callers calling in and saying how hot our song was. Kaiden and I dapped each other up, barely being able to contain all of the excitement that roared inside of us.

"Congratulations, boys, you guys just became local celebrities!" He said with a chuckle. We stayed until the broadcast was over and talked with the DJ. He told us he would be spinning at a night club after he left the station and invited us to join him. That night we partied to the wee hours of the morning. We made use of our newfound celebrity and received so much love that night. As the drinks flowed and the girls shook their waistlines, we partied as we had already become super rap stars.

When I got home the next day, it was early afternoon. I reminisced on the night before. I hadn't thought about the fight between Mona and Kia since I had gone to the radio station the night before. I would be reminded of the bout once I stepped inside the house. "Where have you been all damn night!?" my father growled at me as I handed him over the keys to his car. "I know, dad, I should have called, but it was so late when I remembered to—" "Next time, call anyway. Your mother was worried. By the way, Kia's mother has called for you twice." I stopped dead in my tracks on the way to my bedroom. "She said something about pressing charges on Mona." My dad said as I made my way back into the living room. I knew I had to face the situation finally, and my father was the right person to seek advice from. After I gave him detail after detail, he sat for a minute before he finally said, "That was pretty dumb of you, boy." Shaking his head at the idea of me taking my girlfriend to my ex-girlfriend's house. "What were you thinking?" "I told you I didn't want her to think I was hiding something from her." I said, all the while seeing how dumb that idea was. "Call Kia's mother and apologize for causing this to happen. Then call Mona and tell her about the warrant." My dad offered as he got up from his chair and placed his hand on my shoulder. "Oh, and your car privileges are suspended for two weeks." He said reluctantly as he walked away, leaving me my phone calls.

After receiving my verbal ass whooping from Kia's mom, it was a lot easier to call Mona and tell her about the warrant that Kia's mother had put out on her. "You really fucked up this time." I said before telling her the bad news. She was in tears when we got off the phone. With my car privileges taken away, it would be a nice little break from her, I thought, as I hung up the phone. Besides, I had the essay to write for the scholarship, exams, and the practice SAT coming up, and the Black History program. Not to mention my regular homework that wouldn't wait. At least I was able to celebrate in true form last night, I thought, as I decided to get a head start on my assignments.

Chapter 17 My First Writings

I decided to take a break from smoking weed for a while. There were too many things that required my brain cells. I chuckled at the thought of my schoolwork becoming a priority over selling dope, writing raps, and dare I say, smoking herb, but it had, at least, temporarily. For the next three weeks, I took the deep plunge into my studies. I would call Mona after school to check up on her and let her know I missed her. She had turned herself in, and in court was given two months of community service as punishment for fighting Kia. For a pregnant girl, that would be picking up trash at the city park. I missed her. However, I enjoyed the much needed break my punishment brought us. At school, I was walking tall, feeling like the man. The radio station had put our song in their everyday rotation. Kaiden and I were already popular seniors, with a hot rap song on the radio, we had everyone's support and attention at our school. The producer of our song was just as excited as we were. His project studio went from having two clients to twenty after our song got played. Kaiden sent word from him that we had to get back in the studio soon.

One night, as I sat at my desk to start writing for the essay, all the memories of hustling, stealing, fighting, and just being downright stupid poured in from the depths of my mind. I hadn't thought about death in a while. I started my paper with little anecdotes about my days and nights in the streets and finished it up by stating how much I had changed for the better after seeing the error in my ways. The essay exceeded the required five hundred words. I imagined the reactions of the judges who would be choosing the composition that would earn the scholarship. I had penned an excellent swan song of an essay. I stacked several sheets of paper together and left them out for my mother to read when she got home from work.

With only four months left until graduation, I couldn't help but feel optimistic about the future. At such an early age, I had taken off headfirst in the wrong direction. Now I was power walking down the right path. For a seventeen-year-old, I had experienced a lot. It had never occurred to me that I hadn't thought about what it would be like to be eighteen. "Classes are starting to come into the auditorium now." A teacher said to me in the bathroom. I nodded ok, then looked at myself in the mirror one last time to check my drawn-on goatee. I would have to revisit those thoughts of being eighteen at another time. Right now, my thoughts had to be those of Malcolm X. I took full responsibility for delivering his "Ballot or the Bullet" speech with the same passion and zeal he had some decades before. I slid on my dad's reading glasses and was now in character. As I walked out into the auditorium, the low rumble of multiple conversations among the student body gave me some anxiety. I sat down with the rest of the Black History presenters as the program opened up with a negro spiritual sung by the chorus members. After an introduction given by the senior class president, it was my turn at the podium. I leaned into the mic and said, "As Salaam Alaikum." When the famous speech came to an end, the whole school stood and gave me a standing ovation.

After the roar settled down, I could hear Drake in the crowd yell, "That's my cousin!" That afternoon when I got home, I noticed my essay was on the table with a note from my mom attached to it. It read, "I made some changes that are marked in red." As I thumbed through the essay that was now riddled with red ink strikes, I became bothered at my mother's editing ideas. My essay of heartfelt details of my dealings in the streets had been reduced to a false narrative of how I used to be. I was furious with my mother, and I would let her know exactly how much so when she got home that night from work. "Ma." I said as calmly as I could as she walked in from her twelve-hour shift. "What are you still doing up?"

she said, looking relieved to be home from work finally. "I needed to talk to you about my essay." I said with the tone of an E flat. "You changed so much of it...it has become something that I know wouldn't even compete." My mother took a seat at the dining room table as I went on and on about how she had left out all the critical parts. "You need to listen to me!" she said sharply. "The winning essay will be printed in the newspaper. You don't need to tell all your business for people to see and pass judgment on us." She said jestingly. "Us?" I snapped back at her. "The essay is about me, not about us." I said pleadingly. "Not everyone needs to know how —" she paused. "How what, Ma?" I said, picking up her words. "How bad I was?" I stormed out of the dining room and into my bedroom. I was pissed with her but wasn't foolish enough to slam my door. The next morning, I had the bright idea to take my essay and submit it anyway. When I went to get it off the table, it was gone. In its place was the water-downed version my mother had typed up overnight. I left it there on the table and headed out for school. I got halfway through the day before fate would have me bump right into Ms. Howard. "Hey, I was hoping I would see you today." She said in her usual sing-song voice. "Do you have your essay ready to submit?" She asked. I couldn't maintain eye contact with her, knowing I was about to let her down. "I don't Ms. Howard...my mother and I had some...differences in writing styles you see." I said, trying to explain away my not submitting the winning essay she knew I had written. "I see. That is unfortunate." She said slowly. We stood there for a minute in uncomfortable silence. "See you around, Ms. Howard." I said, filling the silence with words so I could depart. She placed a hand on my shoulder and said, "Ok." I walked away knowing that Ms. Howard knew that my essay would've gotten me that scholarship, but also, there was a chance my story could have helped other kids who had the Grim Reaper on their heels.

The spring of '97 came with the usual senior activities. There was the prom, several dances, senior trip, and the senior photos that I used my local celebrity to stunt to the maximum. Kaiden and I decided our next track would be an ode to those who had died, after hearing the news that the Notorious B.I.G. had been fatally shot down on March 9 after the Soul Train Music Awards. Tupac Shakur had been killed just months before, so it was only right. We had lost several schoolmates as well to various causes, so the more we wrote, the more significant the song became. I had a hard time writing my sixteen bars for the song we called "Gone but not Forgotten." After a couple of rewrites, I decided to write about Tyler and the drive-by and put off writing my contribution to the song for later. It had been a whole year since I had been uptown, and the allure of the lawlessness beckoned me to come and see about her. I ran into Radio at the pool hall as I was entering, and he was leaving. We shared some crazy re-up stories. One was when we were getting dope from some connects from a nearby city. We were the out of towners at that junction, so Radio let me carry his TEC 9 assault rifle on me as we made the transaction. "What's up, Radio!" I said, slapping my hand into his for the exchange of a dap. "What's up, my nigga!" He said, mirroring my excitement. "Where the hell you been at?" We left the pool hall and went over to this feinds house. He setup the little shotgun house as his place of business. The tenants were this crackhead couple, who had crackhead friends that would come over to party how crackheads party. It made sense for Radio to have chosen this spot. When we entered the house, he made himself at home and told me to do the same. We sat and smoked, then reminisced about our adventures on the block.

Midway of our conversation, the woman that lived there came through the door. "What's up, kid?" She said to me, offering her hand for dap. She reeked of beer and cigarettes.

"What's up—" I said, pausing as I caught myself almost slipping and calling her "Bulldog." Bulldog was a name given to her as she looked like a British bulldog in the face, but a British bulldog was prettier. She hated the name and would curse up a storm at anyone that would call her that except for anyone who was supplying her high.

"Bulldog...you supposed to have been here by now!" Radio said as he finished rolling up the next blunt. "Ok, it's coming, motherfucker, give me a minute." She said sheepishly, washing her hands. I sat back and watched the two of them work themselves into an argument. It came to me all of a sudden.

My eyes were now open to how cocaine numbs the brain. Here they were—a drug dealer and a drug addict, trying to one-up each other. "Here's your food, motherfucker!" Bulldog said as she hovered over Radio with a piping hot bowl of chili. As I took one last tote of the blunt before passing it off to Radio, I noticed the pregnant silence they finally had between them. I was grateful. Their bickering was blowing my high. When Radio took the blunt from me, he stared up at her briefly, then knocked the bowl from her hands. The bowl somersaulted through the air somehow and somehow kept its contents intact. I blew out the last of the chronic smoke as my eyes followed the descent of the bowl filled with steaming hot chili as it landed atop Bulldog's head. As she stood there in total awe and shock, she resembled a little bulldog pup that had turned over its dinner bowl on itself. The irony of it all led Radio and me to burst into uncontrollable laughter. We were hysterical, still passing around the good cheba. Through the side-splitting laugh fest, I managed to say, "Bulldog, are you ok?" This enraged her further as she took off back to the kitchen, retrieving a butcher's knife. Radio and I both continued to laugh as we ran out of the house into the night, falling along the way, as Bulldog cursed us from the doorsteps. It took us a minute to calm down long enough to talk normally. "Oh, man! My head hurts from laughing so hard." I said as we walked the backstreet back to my house.

"Hell yea, man. She is mad as hell right now." Radio said nonchalantly. "Yo, I wanted to tell you that I was getting out the game." I said as my words trailed off in the night air. I knew all too well what he was thinking. "Good for you, motherfucker!" Here I was, some middle-class kid, who had only played in the very decay he had to live in, standing there telling him that I had a choice and that I choose not to do what he had no choice in doing. "Stay right here, and I'll be right back." I ran inside my house, got an old bookbag, stuffed the triple beam scale inside it, and rejoined Radio out in the street. As I approached, he lit up the blunt from earlier and said, "Yo, I'm glad you're getting out." I looked at him confused as he continued. "You're different; book smart and street smart." I took the blunt from him and let his words bury their way into my memory. "Do something with that shit." He said, giving me a look of seriousness. "I will." I said, returning the sincerity of his words. "Here, this is for you." I said, giving him a dap, then turning around walking toward my house. "Tools of the trade." I replied. "Tools of the trade."

Mona gave birth to our daughter only days before my graduation commencement. There are no words to describe how soul-stirring it was to hold her in my arms for the first time. My daughter was all the inspiration I needed to change my life around. What a ride the last nine years of my experience had been. It all seemed so distant now, feeling like a lifetime ago. That night at graduation, as I waited for my name to be called to receive my diploma, I thought about the future. What now, what's next? I was awakened from my daydream when my name was called over the loudspeakers.

I brushed off my cap and gown and headed over to where our principal stood. I took my diploma in one hand and shook the principle's hand with the other. "Smile, son...you made it!" he said as if he knew how true of a statement he had made. His words drew the biggest smile on my face. "Yes...I did, didn't I?" As I walked back to my seat with the diploma in hand, I took one last look around. Kenny Sutherland and I made eye contact. We gave one another a head nod as I took my seat beside Drake. After all this time, the Grim Reaper was no longer in sight or mind. I like to think his absence was his way of saying, "You're welcome." The End.

www.ingramcontent.com/pod-product-compliance
Lightning Source LLC
Chambersburg PA
CBHW072005090426
42740CB00011B/2100